Jermyn.

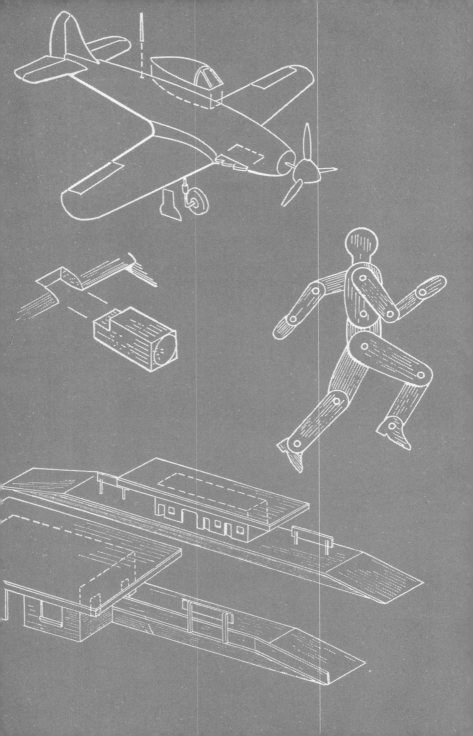

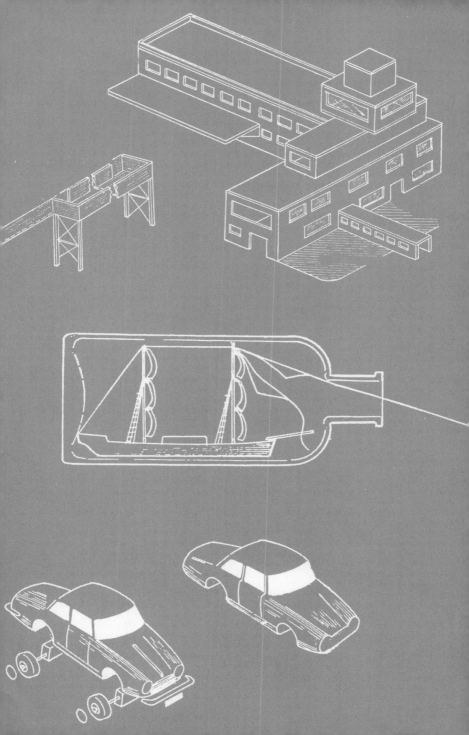

scale models in balsa

Taplinger's Teach-Yourself-Crafts Series

Taking Up Drawing and Painting
Taking Up Sculpture
Scale Models in Balsa

A. M. Colbridge

scale models in balsa

TAPLINGER PUBLISHING COMPANY | NEW YORK

First published in the United States in 1972 by
TAPLINGER PUBLISHING CO., INC.
New York, New York

Library of Congress Catalog Card Number: 72-2196

ISBN 0-8008-6999-0 (Cloth Edition)

ISBN 0-8008-7000-X (Paper Edition)

Contents

Note to American Readers

The following terms may be unfamiliar to some American readers and are accordingly clarified to facilitate the use of this book:

Perspex——Lucite
Saloon——Sedan

scale models in balsa

1 About Scale Models

A scale model is a reproduction, to reduced size, of some object. The amount of reduction is called the 'scale'. 'Model' implies that it is a miniature or smaller version of something, although the description 'miniature' is only correct where a small scale is being used. A scale model of a liner built to a length of, say, 12 inches, when the full size liner is 1000 feet long, is to a scale of 1/1000th. Because this is a very small scale this would also qualify as a 'miniature'. A scale model of a car or an aeroplane, on the other hand, may be as large as 1/12th, or even 1/6th. It is still a scale model, but no longer a true 'miniature'. Sometimes, indeed, the reproduction is as large as the original subject – scale 1/1, or full size. In that case it is no longer a scale model but a *mock-up*. Mock-ups are made to check shapes, plan interior layouts, etc., in full size aircraft and car designs; and for making glass fibre moulds.

Scale models may also be classified in other ways. The majority are scale in appearance only. The way they are made, and the materials from which they are constructed, are quite different from those of the full size object. The plastic kit model is a typical example of a scale model in appearance.

At the other extreme we find elaborate built-up scale models of steam locomotives, traction engines, and so on, which are actually made from similar materials, and in the same manner as the full size subject, and even work in the same way. These are *true working scale models,* within the limits of the materials used. They are also the most exacting to make and a single model of this type may take years to complete.

In between there are a whole lot of different possibilities. The model which is scale in appearance only may be given working features to make it more attractive or realistic. It may also be designed and built throughout as a *working* model, using different materials and simplified construction. In this case it is really an *outline* scale model. The outline or shape is to true scale, but everything inside the outline is designed and built in modelling materials, using modelling techniques. These may or may not also attempt to give a scale appearance to the structure.

For example, take a *working* scale model aeroplane – or *flying scale model,* as it would normally be called. In order to make a successful *flying* model, balsa would normally be chosen for the material to build it from. If the model is fairly small, probably most of the parts could be cut from sheet balsa, as in figure 1.1.

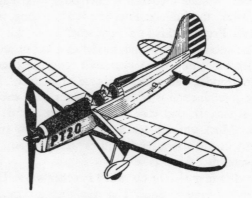

Figure 1.1 All-balsa semi-scale flying model

This would give a model true in outline and overall appearance, but with a structure quite different from that of the full size aeroplane.

The alternative is to duplicate the built-up framework of the original aircraft in parts cut from balsa sheet and strip. This scale-type structure is then covered in tissue (representing fabric covering) and thin balsa sheet (representing ply or thin metal). Again the structure has been kept light enough to make it a flying model.

Both types are, in fact, flying scale models. In the one case the construction has been simplified. In other words it has been designed as a 'model' rather than a 'replica'. It will appeal more to the person who wants 'working' results and does not want to spend too much time on construction. The other has been built up in the manner of a full size aeroplane. Because of its more complicated construction it will probably be heavier and not fly so well. But it will appeal more to the person who gets most enjoyment from the actual *construction* of scale models, rather than having them work.

Where the emphasis is on 'working' rather than 'true scale', too, the modeller may have to cheat a little. He may use built-up construction for lightness, but very much simplified. The overall appearance will then be more like that of a flying model rather than a true scale model, although the outline shape may be to scale. He may also have to cheat on the outline as well to produce a model which flies satisfactorily, such as using larger-than-scale tailplane and fin sizes. If this is carried too far the result is no longer a scale model but one which is more properly called a *semi-scale* model. But it still looks like a 'scale' model of 'full size' aircraft, and is instantly recognizable as such (figure 1.2).

Figure 1.2 Semi-scale flying model aircraft

What all this really means is that in scale modelling there is scope to choose different types of approach, depending on what you want from the model. Construction can be simplified to a degree, if you want results with a minimum of time spent on actual construction. It is here that balsa wood is particularly valuable as a modelling material, because of the ease with which it can be worked – see Chapter 2. This applies equally well to simple 'model' constructions, to true 'scale type' structures, and to many subjects other than aircraft, as will be explained in the following chapters.

Scales

The choice of scale is largely a matter of convenience. Basically, what would be the most suitable size for the model? This depends on several things – how big the full size subject is; what type of model is to be built; and whether it is to be one of a collection of models or not. Individual models are usually best built to a fairly large scale. This justifies the amount of work put into them, and makes a more impressive model. It is also easier to add more realistic detail, adding to their scale appearance. Models forming part of a collection should be built to a *standard* scale, so that each one is true to size compared with the others.

Standard scales are those commonly adopted for producing commercial scale models of various types, and generally followed by individual modellers. The following are the standard scales in general use, but this does not mean that all commercial models are produced to one of these specific scales. Some are produced to odd scales, close to a standard scale. Starting with the smallest scale first, there is:

Figure 1.3 Waterline scale model ship

1/1200th scale This is often used for small waterline ship models, since it gives a length of about 10 to 12 inches for a large liner, or tanker. It is really too small a scale for modelling a fleet of ships. A tug, for example, would be about 1 inch long to this scale, which leaves little scope for detail. It is an easy scale to work out since 1 inch equals 100 feet. In other words, the full size dimension, in feet, divided by 100, gives the corresponding scale dimension in inches. You would thus work with an inch rule, subdivided into *tenths*, or preferably *fiftieths* of an inch (subdivisions of 1/100th inch would be too close together to read properly).

1/1000th scale This is an alternative to 1/1200th scale for large ship subjects, but not so easy to work out. You have to divide the full size dimension by 1000 and then multiply by 12 to get the scale dimension in inches.

Figure 1.4 Full-depth scale model ship

1/600th scale Again used for ship models, and ideal for use with an inch rule subdivided into *fiftieths*. The scale dimension in inches is given by dividing the full size dimension by 50. It is often quicker to do this calculation by multiplying the full size dimension in feet by 2 and then dividing by 100.

Various intermediate scales from 1/600th down may be used

for ship models and models of other large subjects, but the next usual one is:

000 gauge or 'N' gauge This is a scale adopted for model railways only and is equivalent to 2 millimetres equalling 1 foot. It is close enough to 1/144th scale to be regarded as almost identical for the purpose of 'matched' collections.

1/144th scale This corresponds to 1 inch equals 12 feet. In this case work with an inch rule subdivided into *twelfths*. Dividing the full size dimension in feet by 12 then gives the scale dimension in inches and twelfths of an inch. 1/144th scale is mainly used for less detailed models of large aircraft or similar large full size subjects.

1/96th scale This corresponds to 1 inch equals 8 feet. Dividing the full size dimension by 8 will give the scale dimension in inches and eighths of an inch. An inch rule subdivided into eighths is thus used when working with this scale. 1/96th scale is used for larger aircraft prototypes.

TT gauge This is a standard model railway scale, equivalent to 2.5 or 3 millimetres equalling 1 foot. It is virtually the same as 1/96th scale.

1/72nd scale This is the most common scale for non-working scale model aircraft, including plastic kits, and is a very convenient scale for collections of models all to the same scale. Since 1 inch equals 6 feet in this scale, dividing the full size dimension in feet by 6 will give the corresponding scale dimension in inches and sixths of an inch. Use an inch rule subdivided into twelfths. Each 1/12th of an inch will then represent 1/2 foot or 6 inches, full size.

HO gauge This is another standard model railway scale given by 3.5 millimetres equalling 1 foot. It is a little smaller than 1/72nd scale, but is a suitable match in a mixed collection.

OO gauge This standard model railway scale is based on 4 millimetres equalling 1 foot. It is almost exactly equivalent to 1/72nd scale.

1/48th scale This is a convenient scale for larger non-working scale models of aircraft and cars, enabling much more detail to be incorporated than on 1/72nd scale models. The scale is

Figure 1.5 Galleon model with solid hull and built-up superstructure

equivalent to 1/4 inch equalling 1 foot. Thus, dividing the full size dimension in feet by 4 gives the scale dimension in inches and quarters of an inch. Work with a standard inch rule subdivided into *sixteenths*.

1/36th scale This enables even better detail to be incorporated on the model than 1/48th scale. Dividing the full size dimension in feet by 3 gives the scale dimension in inches and thirds of an inch. Normal rules are not subdivided in multiples of thirds, but *twelfth* subdivisions can be used, remembering that each subdivision then represents 3 inches to scale. For a collection this scale has the disadvantage that models of larger prototypes can be huge – for example, a 200-ft wingspan bomber would be over $5\frac{1}{2}$ feet in model size.

0 gauge This is another standard railway scale, almost exactly the same as 1/36th scale. The actual scale is 7 millimetres to the foot.

1/32nd scale This scale is commonly adopted for car models. It

Figure 1.6 Model houses are another ideal subject for modelling in balsa

is a little awkward to work with for 3/8 inch equals 1 foot. In other words, using an inch rule with *eighth* subdivisions, each subdivision would equal 4 inches (or with *sixteenth* subdivisions each subdivision would equal 2 inches).

1/24th scale This is a fairly large scale used for individual *working* models of aircraft and cars. Since 1/2 inch equals 1 foot, it is a very easy scale to work with.

1/12th scale In this case 1 inch equals 1 foot, so if you work with an inch ruler subdivided into *twelfths*, each subdivision represents 1 inch. 1/12th scale is used for larger flying scale model aircraft and working scale model boats.

1/6th scale Used for really large flying scale model aircraft, usually radio-controlled. In this case 2 inches equals 1 foot, so an inch ruler subdivided into twelfths would mean that each subdivision was equal to 1/2 inch.

Note: In the case of model railway scales, different scales are sometimes used for the *track* and the superstructure of the rolling stock. Thus HO and OO scales may be mixed; also TT gauge may be true 2.5mm to the foot scale throughout, or employ rolling stock with superstructures to 3mm to the foot scale running on 2.5mm to the foot scale track. Rolling stock to HO gauge (3.5mm to the foot) may also be used on OOO or or 'N' gauge track (2mm to the foot). In this case the combination is usually referred to as 'HO9'.

Choice of Scale

Choice of scale should normally be based on suitable standard scales. There is no reason why individual models cannot be made to any scale desired, however. What really matters is that the model should be a suitable size to suit the purpose for which it is intended. One general rule which can be applied here is that in the case of *working* models, the larger the scale the better. Against this must be considered the following facts:

1 Size may be restricted by convenience. A very large model will be awkward to store and difficult to transport.

2 The larger the model the more it will cost in terms of both materials and time. Doubling the size of a model from, say, 1/24th scale to 1/12th scale will require *eight* times the amount of material.

Rules for Detail

Choice of scale will also govern the amount of detail which can be incorporated on a scale model while still retaining a realistic appearance.

There is one general rule which can be applied here. The amount of detail which shows on a scale model should be *the same as you would expect to see on the full size subject viewed from such a distance that it looks the same size as the model.* If detail stands out too boldly on a scale model it will look unrealistic. Lack of detail, on the other hand, will make the model

Figure 1.7 Sheet balsa 'box' construction can be used for lineside models built to match model railway scales

look just like a model rather than a proper miniature.

Too much detail, and particularly detail which is out of scale, is worse than lack of detail. This was a common fault on many early plastic kit models. The mouldings were over detailed, with rivet heads showing which, to true scale, were perhaps

Table 1: Summary of Scales

'Inch' scales	*Metric scales*	*Decimal scales*
$\frac{1}{1200}$		
		$\frac{1}{1000}$
$\frac{1}{800}$	0.5mm to 1ft	$\frac{1}{600}$
		$\frac{1}{500}$
$\frac{1}{300}$	1 mm to 1ft	$\frac{1}{300}$
$\frac{1}{240}$		$\frac{1}{250}$
	1.5mm to 1ft	$\frac{1}{200}$
$\frac{1}{144}$	2 mm to 1ft	$\frac{1}{150}$
$\frac{1}{120}$	2.5mm to 1ft	
$\frac{1}{96}$	3 mm to 1ft	$\frac{1}{100}$
	3.5mm to 1ft	$\frac{1}{90}$
$\frac{1}{72}$	4 mm to 1ft	
$\frac{1}{48}$	7 mm to 1ft	$\frac{1}{50}$
		$\frac{1}{40}$
$\frac{1}{36}$	8 mm to 1ft	
$\frac{1}{32}$		$\frac{1}{30}$
$\frac{1}{24}$		$\frac{1}{25}$
		$\frac{1}{20}$
$\frac{1}{18}$		
$\frac{1}{12}$		
		$\frac{1}{10}$
$\frac{1}{8}$		
		$\frac{1}{5}$
$\frac{1}{4}$		
$\frac{1}{2}$		
$\frac{1}{1}$		$\frac{1}{1}$

Note: scales on the same line are approximate equivalents

several inches across and an inch or more high, when the actual rivet head they were meant to represent was less than a 1/4" diameter. Rivets big enough to hold a bridge together showing on a scale model aeroplane!

2 Balsa Wood for Modelling

Balsa is a first choice material for modelling of all kinds, and specially suitable for the simple construction of scale models. Balsa is a natural wood, which means that models built from it are strong and rigid. It is not as strong as other woods, but this is a small price to pay for the fact that balsa is so much easier to cut and shape, and also to join with quick-drying cement (balsa cement). It is also readily available in a wide range of sizes, specially cut for modelling purposes. You can buy balsa in almost all these sizes at any model shop. A more limited range of sizes is also often stocked by do-it-yourself shops, especially in towns which are not served by a separate model shop.

All of the world's supply of balsa wood comes from Ecuador. The balsa tree grows rapidly, developing a long but relatively thin trunk which is cut up into short lengths as soon as a tree is felled. Thus balsa is never available in longer lengths than about 3 feet, nor in widths much greater than about 6 inches. In fact, the standard length for all cut balsa supplies in this country is 36 inches; and the maximum width normally available in either sheet or block form is 4 inches.

Standard cut sizes of balsa are shown in Table 2, p 29. These are generally described as *strip* (up to $1'' \times \frac{1}{2}''$ section); *sheet*, with a normal standard width of $3''$ (but also in $2''$ and $4''$ widths) in thicknesses from $1/32$ inch up to $1/2$ inch; and *block* or solid sections up to $3'' \times 4''$.

These standard sizes cover the majority of modelling requirements. If larger widths or sections are required it is an easy matter to join standard pieces together by gluing, when the joint strength will be at least as good as that of the wood itself if properly made. This is far simpler, and cheaper, than trying to obtain special sizes of balsa.

If *strip* lengths longer than the standard 36 inches are required, then two (or more) separate lengths of strip should be cemented together with a *scarf joint* (see figure 2.1). This joint

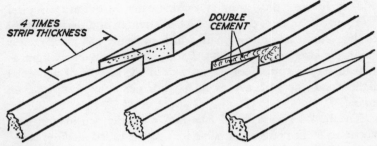

Figure 2.1

needs cutting very accurately, preferably with a razor saw, and should be double cemented for strength. The joint will then be stronger than the balsa section itself.

Where *sheet* lengths longer than 36 inches are required, individual sheets should be butt jointed (figure 2.2). If this joint cannot be supported by a frame member behind it, then it should be strengthened with a butt strap cemented on the back face over the joint. The butt strap can be of the same thickness as the sheet jointed and needs to be about 1 inch wide. Additional *width* of sheet can be produced by cementing up two sheets edge

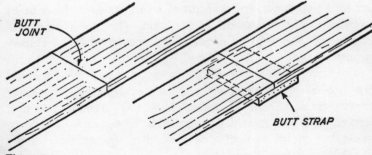

Figure 2.2

to edge. In this case no butt strap will be required. The joint should be strong enough on its own if double cemented.

Balsa Grades and Cuts

Mainly because they grow at varying rates in different tropical weathers, balsa trees can vary a lot in strength and density. Balsa is thus unlike any other wood, which normally has more or less the same strength and weight. Balsa, in fact, can be as light as 6 pounds per cubic foot (about a fifth the weight of a normal light wood), or as heavy as 20 pounds per cubic foot, or even more.

The bulk of balsa wood falls into a middle density range of about 10 to 12 pounds per cubic foot, and is called *medium balsa*. Both lighter and heavier balsa may also be available, the former generally called *soft balsa*, and the latter *hard balsa*.

Medium balsa is suitable for most modelling purposes. Where light construction is important, however, *soft* balsa may be preferred, especially for parts carved from solid block. Soft balsa is also easier to carve than heavier balsa. If strength is more important, then *hard* balsa can be used – such as for spars and load-carrying members in built-up frames.

Such different weights or grades are not marked on the balsa, although grading by density is always done at the factory where balsa lumber is received. It is then further selected to reject pieces which may be faulty or unsuitable for modelling. Selection of individual pieces of soft, medium or hard is then left to the customer, and with practice this can easily be done by 'weighing' different pieces in the hand. The model shop proprietor can also help in selecting a particular grade or density required.

The 'cut' is rather a different matter. Depending on the way the original log is sawn up into smaller sections, the annual growth rings will lie in various directions through the final section. This is not normally significant in the case of strip or block, but in the case of sheet will affect the stiffness of the sheet. Here three different types of 'cut' can be identified.

Most sheets will be produced by random cutting, which will produce a sheet which is slightly bendable from edge to edge, and also from end to end (figure 2.3). If the cut is slightly different,

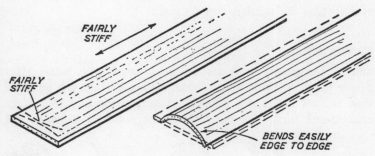

FAIRLY STIFF

FAIRLY STIFF

BENDS EASILY EDGE TO EDGE

Figure 2.3

however, the sheet may be stiff from end to end, but bend readily from edge to edge. It is difficult to distinguish between the two 'cuts' without actually trying the pieces for 'bendability'. Both will have a normal straight-grained appearance on the surface, but one will be very much more bendable edge-to-edge than the other. This may perhaps occur only in one piece in a dozen or more, but is the sort of sheet which would be picked out for using to cover curved surfaces. For most other work the ordinary, stiffer sheet would be used.

The third type of cut is readily distinguished by the speckled appearance of the grain on the surface of the sheet (figure 2.4). This is called quarter-grain or quarter-sawn sheet and is very

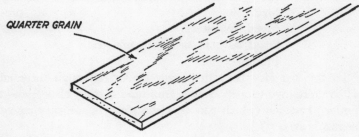

QUARTER GRAIN

Figure 2.4

stiff from edge to edge. If you try to bend it that way it will split instead of bending. This is the sort of sheet which would be selected for making members which have to be stiff and rigid. Again it will appear far less regularly in a random stock collection of sheet than the ordinary straight grain.

Cutting balsa

Only a few simple tools are needed to work with balsa. Most people prefer to work with a modelling knife which can be fitted with various blades for different cutting work, and also other attachments such as a razor saw. The number of blades and

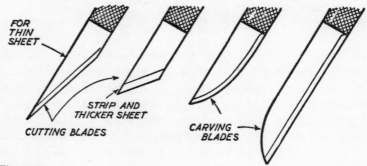

Figure 2.5

attachments required can be reduced to a minimum, as shown in figure 2.5, although others may be invaluable for certain types of work (e.g., gouges for carving).

In addition the following tools must be regarded as essential:

Steel rule
Metal square
Small dovetail saw with fine teeth
Fretsaw

To this list may be added razor blades (although these are really alternative to a modelling knife and cutting blade); and a 'junior' hacksaw (which can take the place of, or supplement, the razor saw).

Most sizes of sheet and strip can be cut with a knife. Block is also carved with a knife, but best cut to shape with a saw. The one essential thing is that all cutting edges must be really sharp. Although balsa is soft and easy to cut, the fibres do have a dulling effect on knife edges, and once the edge has lost its keenness it will tear rather than cut the wood. Razor blades should be thrown away once they have lost their sharpness. Knife blades are rather too expensive to discard immediately they show signs of becoming blunt, so an oilstone should be added to the tool kit on which blades can be resharpened. There is a special knack to this, which takes practice and time to learn.

Strip balsa up to about 3/16″ square can be cut to length with a modelling knife or razor blade. Larger strip sections, especially in hard balsa, are best cut with a razor saw (or 'junior' hacksaw) (figure 2.6). This will give a neater and easier cut than

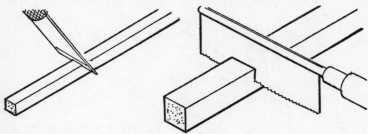

Figure 2.6

a knife, and save blunting the knife.

Parts can be cut out from *sheet balsa* with a modelling knife in all thicknesses up to about 1/4 inch. Straight cuts should always be guided by a metal rule. Curved cuts will have to be made freehand (figure 2.7). The thicker the sheet the more difficult it will be to keep the knife upright to produce a 'square' cut. Also the more important it will be that the knife really is sharp, especially for clean cutting across the grain of the wood.

There will come a point where the sheet is either too thick, or too hard, to be cut accurately with a knife. In this case a saw must be used – a razor saw for straight cuts, or a fretsaw for curved cuts. Again it is important to keep the saw vertical so that the cut is 'square'.

Figure 2.7

Where the part required has a piece cut out of its centre, this should be cut first. To avoid 'nicking' the corners, which would weaken the final piece, all cuts should be made *away* from sharp corners. Thus figure 2.8 shows the sequence of making cuts to remove the centre from a marked out piece. After this

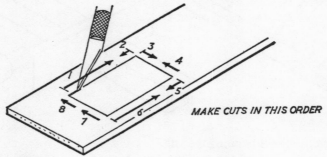

Figure 2.8

centre has been removed, the final piece can be cut out. It often helps to replace the cut out piece temporarily to give support to the rest of the sheet at this stage.

To cut block balsa to length, the length required should be marked off, and then carried round all four faces, using a metal square and pencil or ball point pen, as shown in figure 2.9. The block can then be cut with a dovetail saw, checking that the cut proceeds correctly down the marked line.

Further treatment of block shapes is dealt with in more detail

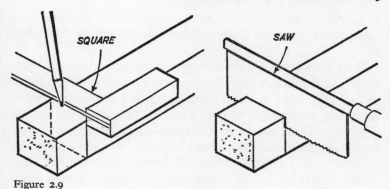

Figure 2.9

in Chapters 4 and 7, describing the making of solid scale models. The basic procedure in such cases is that the block is first *sawn* to a blank shape, and the blank then *carved* down to the final shape, using a carving blade (figure 2.5).

Glued joints

The standard glue for balsa is balsa cement, which is a very fast-drying adhesive. It sets in a few minutes, and the joint is quite hard in half an hour or so.

For an ordinary join, coating one piece of balsa and bringing it in place to close the joint is sufficient. The two parts must then be held tightly together until the cement has set. The easiest way to do this is usually to stick pins through one piece into the other. Balsa is soft enough to take pins easily, without damage to the wood, except in the case of very small strip sections. Here it may be necessary to locate the pins on either side of the piece rather than through it; or use rubber bands to clamp in position. Provided such a joint is properly closed – that is, the two pieces are brought together under some pressure with a film of balsa cement between them – the resulting joint should be as strong as the wood.

For an even stronger joint, or to make sure that the joint is not 'dry', double-cementing can be used. This consists of coating *each* joint surface lightly with cement and allowing this to set for perhaps a minute. Each surface is then re-coated with cement, the joint closed and clamped or pinned up tight until set.

Balsa cement can be used for almost all balsa gluing jobs, but there are the exceptions. Where large areas have to be joined at one time, such as sheet covering applied over a framework, or gluing fairly large blocks together, PVA or white glue is generally a better adhesive. It is much slower setting, so it gives more 'shuffling time' for completing the joint and avoids any possibility of the glue setting off before the joint has been closed. PVA is also a very 'clean' glue as surplus adhesive which has oozed out of joint lines can be wiped off without staining the wood. Surplus balsa cement sets in hard blobs which are difficult to remove.

Because of its clean working properties, some modellers prefer PVA or white glue to balsa cement for all work. However, it does have the disadvantage of taking ten hours or more to set, so that joints have to be left clamped or pinned up for that time at least (preferably overnight). Also PVA cannot be used if the joints are to be waterproof, as for example in the construction of scale model boats which are to float.

Even balsa cement is not fully waterproof, although it is near enough so for all practical purposes with balsa to balsa joints. It does not, however, produce a waterproof joint for gluing balsa to other woods or ply. In such cases a synthetic resin glue must be used, such as Cascamite or Aerolite. Either of these adhesives is also preferred for making permanent joints in large balsa blocks to be joined together by gluing.

Painting and finishing balsa

Balsa can be sanded to as smooth a finish as can be obtained with other woods. The surface is, however, soft and porous. As soon as you start to paint it the paint is absorbed and dries out in uneven patches. At the same time the grain is pulled up, so that the surface is roughened.

To avoid this the surface must be *sealed* before applying

any final paint finish. Balsa wood sealers, or sanding sealers as they are usually called, usually consist of clear cellulose or model aircraft dope mixed with talc. They can be bought ready made, or you can mix talc with clear dope yourself to make up any quantity of sealer required. The mixture should be quite thin so that it will sink well into the surface of the wood.

The first application of sealer, which is best brushed on, will roughen the surface of balsa when dry. This should be sanded down smooth again and another coat of sealer applied and allowed to dry. This operation should be repeated as many times as necessary to achieve a really smooth and uniform surface. It should feel as smooth as glass when rubbed over with the finger-tips, and show no rough patches.

It may need as many as six to eight coats of sealer, rubbed down between each coat, to achieve a perfect surface finish, which can then be finally covered with any dope or paint finish. The final colouring coats are best applied by spray rather than brush. To get the highest possible gloss, these can be rubbed down between each coat and after the final coat, and burnished and polished to bring up the final gloss. The time taken to achieve a perfect finish, allowing for drying time between each coat, can be longer than that taken over the construction of the model.

Fortunately there are short cuts for modellers seeking quicker and simpler results, and prepared to accept a finish which may be less than perfect.

1 *Polyurethane wood sealer* This is a stronger sealer than ordinary sanding sealer and a single coat, or at most two coats will usually do a satisfactory job of sealing. The grain will be roughened again during drying, so sanding down after sealing is still necessary.

2 *Emulsion paints* Emulsion paints are good sealers for balsa and have less tendency to raise the grain than other types. Emulsion paints may be used both to seal and provide a colour coating in one on many balsa models, where a matt or semi-matt finish is acceptable. Even sanding down may not be necessary between each coat.

3 *Poster colours* These work in a similar manner to emulsion

paints, except that they produce only a matt or non-shiny finish. Also they are not waterproof. They do, however, provide a simple method of finishing balsa models although, like emulsion paints, they add more weight than sanding sealers followed by colour finish.

4 *Cover with tissue* This is mainly restricted to treating fairly flat surfaces, especially large areas of balsa, as it is difficult to cover sharply curved surfaces without introducing wrinkles or joints in the tissue covering which will show. The type of tissue used should be *model aircraft tissue*, preferably applied to the surface with clear dope rather than tissue paste. A suitable technique is to paint the surface of the balsa with clear dope and allow to dry. The tissue is then laid in place and another thin coat of clear dope applied over the tissue to soak through and bond it in place. The application of tissue in this way seals the surface of the balsa and leaves it smooth. No sanding is required. Further coloured coats can then be applied over the tissue, or if minimum weight is the aim, coloured tissue can be used for covering and giving a final coat or two of clear dope, or thin coloured dope.

5 *Cover with decorative papers* Special 'building papers' are produced printed in brick, stone, roof tile patterns, etc., to various scales. These can be used to cover scale buildings, etc., built in balsa. In this case the balsa needs no finishing except for sanding smooth. The papers are then cut to shape and applied directly to the balsa surface with tissue paste or photographic paste, or some similar adhesive.

6 *Cover with film* Special coloured films are available, complete with an adhesive backing, which can be applied directly to balsa to produce a high gloss coloured finish in one operation. Such films are usually laid in place and then ironed down with a warm iron. The heat from the iron activates the adhesive, so that after ironing the film is bonded strongly and permanently to the balsa. Some practice is needed to avoid wrinkles developing in the film as it is being ironed down and the method is best suited to treating large, flat areas. The film will, however, stretch to cover curves, although compound curved shapes are best covered with separate strips of film.

Film coverings are relatively new, and not as yet widely used as a general modelling finish. They do, however, provide the simplest – and quickest – method of producing a high gloss colour finish on balsa and balsa constructions, where the subject is suitable for such treatment. The smoothness of the finish will be as smooth as the original surface of the balsa to which the film is applied. There is no grain-raising effect, but any imperfections in the balsa surface will show through the film, as will any dust trapped between the film and the surface.

Table 2: Standard Sizes of Balsa

36″ length is standard, but 24″ lengths are also produced in each size

Strip balsa	Sheet balsa
$\frac{1}{16}''$ x $\frac{1}{16}''$	$\frac{1}{32}''$ x 2″
$\frac{1}{8}''$ x $\frac{1}{8}''$	$\frac{1}{32}''$ x 3″
$\frac{1}{8}''$ x $\frac{1}{4}''$	$\frac{1}{16}''$ x 2″
$\frac{1}{8}''$ x $\frac{1}{2}''$	$\frac{1}{16}''$ x 3″
$\frac{1}{8}''$ x $\frac{3}{4}''$	$\frac{3}{32}''$ x 2″
$\frac{3}{16}''$ x $\frac{3}{16}''$	$\frac{3}{32}''$ x 3″
$\frac{3}{16}''$ x $\frac{1}{2}''$	$\frac{1}{8}''$ x 2″
$\frac{1}{4}''$ x $\frac{1}{4}''$	$\frac{1}{8}''$ x 3″
$\frac{3}{8}''$ x $\frac{3}{8}''$	$\frac{3}{16}''$ x 2″
$\frac{1}{2}''$ x $\frac{1}{2}''$	$\frac{3}{16}''$ x 3″
$\frac{1}{2}''$ x 1″	$\frac{1}{4}''$ x 2″
	$\frac{1}{4}''$ x 3″
	$\frac{3}{8}''$ x 2″
Block balsa	$\frac{3}{8}''$ x 3″
1″ x 1″	$\frac{1}{2}''$ x 2″
1″ x 1$\frac{1}{2}''$	$\frac{1}{2}''$ x 3″
1″ x 2″	$\frac{3}{4}''$ x 2″
1$\frac{1}{2}''$ x 1$\frac{1}{2}''$	
1$\frac{1}{2}''$ x 2″	
1$\frac{1}{2}''$ x 2$\frac{1}{2}''$	Balsa dowel
2″ x 2″	1$\frac{1}{4}''$ dia.
2″ x 3″	$\frac{7}{8}''$ dia.
3″ x 3″	$\frac{1}{2}''$ dia.

3   Pictures into Plans

An essential part of scale modelling is to have an accurate plan from which to work. The outline accuracy of a scale model cannot be any better than the accuracy of the plan from which it is made. A good plan will also show other shapes and sections, as well as details. All this information is necessary in order to produce a good scale model, but plans alone are not always sufficient. Photographic illustrations of the subject, such as found in books and magazines, can be invaluable for 'filling in' the detail and showing the finished results required. The good scale modeller, therefore, will always collect as much information as he possibly can on the particular subject he is modelling in miniature.

Interest in scale model aircraft and boats is quite well catered for by published plans. The accuracy of most of these plans produced specially for modellers is generally high, and in the case of aircraft they are often particularly well elaborated in detail. The majority are *general arrangement* drawings normally reproduced to 1/72nd scale, although larger scale prints off the original drawings may also be available – e.g., to 1/36th scale. Little more need be said about such published plans except to emphasize that they are not *constructional* plans. In other words they illustrate the subject, not the manner in which it can be made as a scale model.

A more limited range of constructional scale model plans is also available. These plans are essentially individual *designs*, where a modeller has taken a particular subject and designed and built a scale model of that subject. His plan therefore describes how to build that particular model. Its accuracy as a true scale model depends largely on the original designer's treatment of the subject, and his particular skill as a scale modeller. Plans of this type are normally for built-up models, to a larger scale than that covered by general arrangement drawings.

Either type of plan can provide a starting point for a scale modeller, depending on the type of model he wants to make. A general arrangement drawing will give all the information necessary for making a non-working solid model, for example, and will probably be available in the scale required. It can also be used as a basis for making a working model. In this case the original plan will probably have to be scaled up to a larger scale, and the individual modeller will have to work out his own ideas on construction. The scaled up general arrangement drawing will provide only the outline shapes required, and basic information on cross section shapes and detail. The less experienced modeller would almost certainly be better advised to try to find a working model plan already drawn up to a suitable scale, or alternatively a kit. In the latter case, the actual construction of the model will be described in detail on the plan, or in a separate instruction leaflet. Another advantage offered by a kit is that many parts will already be pre-shaped, or die-cut.

The general requirements of scale model aircraft building, and to a lesser extent scale model boats, are thus fairly well covered with 'ready-made' plans and kits; but a certain amount of modelling experience is needed to turn a general arrangement drawing into a plan for a built-up model. Many subjects may necessitate working from scratch, which first means the drawing up of an outline plan to the required scale, working from whatever information is available.

The best starting point is an existing general arrangement drawing as, provided it is accurate, this only involves a re-drawing job, usually scaling up to a suitable size. The ease with which this can be done depends mainly on the 'conversion factor' involved. Thus if a 1/72nd scale drawing of the subject is available and a 1/24th scale model is required, this only involves re-drawing the plan three times as large. Quite often however, the only general arrangement drawing available may be reproduced to an odd scale, or to no specified scale. Then although the basic technique of scaling up the drawing is the same, the method of treatment is a little different. The first thing in any case is to determine the conversion factor involved.

To do this it is necessary to know the actual dimensions of the full size subject. This can be compared with the measured dimension taken off the available scale drawing, and from this the actual scale of the drawing worked out. For simplification it is recommended that all working and measurement should be done in decimal fractions of an inch (using a ruler or scale sub-divided into at least tenths and preferably fiftieths). Alternatively, work in metric measurements (millimetres) throughout.

Suppose, for example, the subject is a ship, and we have a scale drawing available which shows the length of the hull

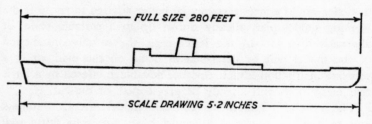

Figure 3.1

as 5.2 inches (figure 3.1). The full size dimension is 280 feet. The actual scale of the drawing is thus:

$$\frac{5.2}{12 \times 280} = \frac{5.2}{3360} = 1/646\text{th}$$

If we want to make a 1/200th scale model, this means that the plan will have to be enlarged in the ratio 646/200, or 3.23 to 1.

Actually there is a simpler way of working out the conversion factor. If the full size dimension is 280 feet and the scale is to be 1/200th, the scale length of the hull would be:

$$\frac{280 \times 12}{200} = \frac{3360}{200} = 16.8 \text{ inches}$$

The scale drawing shows the hull length as 5.2 inches. Therefor the conversion factor for scaling up the plan is:

$$\frac{16.8}{5.2} = 3.23$$

This method of finding the conversion factor is more direct, and less liable to mistakes in calculation.

Now we have an awkward conversion figure to work with. Any measurement taken off the scale drawing must be multiplied by 3.23 to find the corresponding dimension for plotting the 1/200th scale plan wanted. This is very easy if you use a slide rule.

Set the slide of the rule so that the 1 comes against the conversion factor (3.23) on the bottom scale (figure 3.2). Any

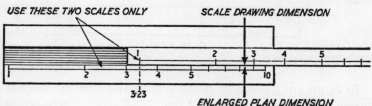

Figure 3.2

dimension taken off the scale drawing and entered on the slide can then be read off as the required dimension for the new plan. It is as simple as that. If the dimension entered on the slide comes off the end of the rule – e.g., 4 would come past the end of the slide rule – move the slide back so that 10 comes against 1 on the body scale.

A slide rule is an invaluable tool for scaling up dimensions in this straightforward way, without calculation. It is not expensive to buy, and no scale modeller who draws up his own plans can really afford to be without one. Some modellers, in fact, buy two slide rules – so that they can set 1 against the conversion factor on one rule, and 10 against the conversion factor on the other, to save changing the slide position from time to time.

With simple whole-number conversion factors you can easily work out the dimensions required. But again a slide rule is simpler and quicker, and avoids any possibility of making a mistake in calculation.

When drawing up scale plans, work from as many full size dimensions as possible. These are worked out to scale and plotted on the drawing, remembering that you need the following views:

Side elevation

Plan

End elevation (or two elevations, one from each end).

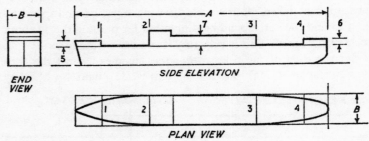

Figure 3.3

In figure 3.3, dimensions A and B are scaled from the full size dimensions available (length and beam). All other dimensions in this case must then be scaled off the smaller drawing available, working step by step, e.g.,

1 length of forecastle
2 start of superstructure from bow
3 end of superstructure from bow
4 start of poop, from stern
5 height of forecastle
6 height of poop
7 height of superstructure, and so on.

This procedure is quite simple when working with straight shapes. For curved shapes it is necessary to divide the length of the shape up into a number of *stations*, as shown in figure 3.4. These can be arranged at convenient spacings. Offset dimensions are then measured about the centreline or datum line and transferred as adjusted measurements to the final scale drawing.

In some cases it is more convenient to plot offsets from an out-

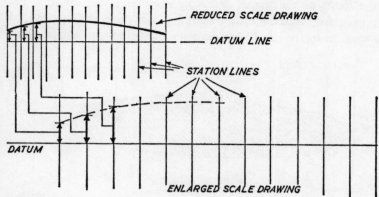

Figure 3.4

side line. Thus figure 3.5 shows the same method applied to
plotting a wing tip shape. In this case the reference line is
drawn as a tangent to the tip shape. Station lines are plotted
as close as necessary to get a good reproduction of the curve.

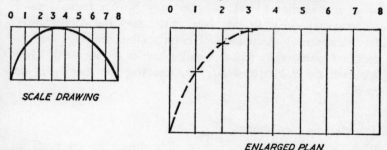

Figure 3.5

Working from photographs

Where no scale drawing of the subject is available, then it may
be necessary to work from photographs. This method is generally
less accurate, as even exact side and head-on photographs are
liable to have some distortion of the true shapes present.

The best than can be done in such cases is to work to full size
dimensions as far as possible, worked out to scale, to establish

the limits of the shape; and scale everything else up from the photograph, marked with a suitable datum line and stations, as shown in figure 3.6. Corrections for perspective, or the fact that

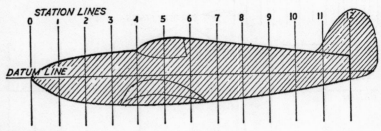

Figure 3.6

a particular part is not a true side elevation view, will have to be estimated. With care and patience, and a study of as many other photographs as possible, a reasonably accurate outline drawing can be prepared in this way.

A scale outline drawing is all that is necessary to make a simple solid or waterline model, provided any further basic detail is incorporated – e.g., a ship plan must show the deck 'layers' (see Chapter 6). A number of cross section drawings are also required, particularly where rounded shapes are involved. These are used for making *templates* for checking the shaping of the model.

Transferring plan shapes

With solid model construction, outline shapes are taken off the plan and transferred on to balsa for cutting out. The more accurately this is done, the better. There are several possible methods, of varying accuracy:

1 *Tracing* This is the most obvious method, copying the outline on tracing paper and then using this, inverted, to trace through on to the balsa. It is the least accurate method because two further drawings are involved, and errors can accumulate.

2 *Pricking through* This again involves making a tracing, but this is simply laid on the balsa the same way up. The outline is

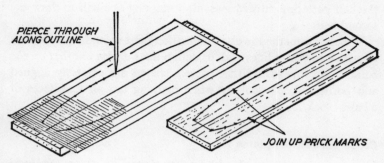

Figure 3.7

then pricked through (figure 3.7). The prick lines are then drawn in to complete the marked out shape. This is more accurate since only one drawing is involved, that of the original tracing.

3 *Cut patterns* Here the traced shape is marked out on to stiff paper which is then cut out to shape. The shape can be checked by laying over the original drawing, and if in error corrected or remade. The pattern is then pinned or held down on the balsa, and drawn around to mark the shape (figure 3.8) Alternatively

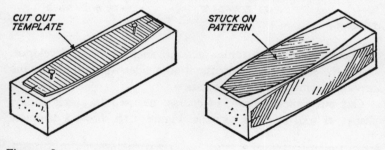

Figure 3.8

the pattern can be cut from thin paper lightly glued down to the balsa, e.g., with rubber gum, and the balsa cut to shape around the pattern. The use of a cut out pattern, which is also known as a template, is usually the most accurate method for marking out solid models. Half patterns can also be used to ensure marking out perfectly symmetrical shapes. In this case the half pattern is turned over after marking one half to draw the second half.

Whichever method is used, all marking out should be done with reference to centre lines and/or datum lines *drawn out first on the balsa*. This will ensure that pattern shapes are correctly aligned and positioned, particularly when marking out all four faces of a balsa block.

Cross section templates

Cross section shapes should be transferred to thick card and then cut out in the form of *half section templates*, as shown in figure 3.9. These can then be offered up as carving proceeds

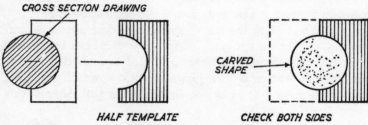

Figure 3.9

to check that the right cross sectional shape is being developed. Using the same template to check both sides will ensure that the carving is symmetrical at that station.

Cut out templates can, of course, be used to check outline shapes as well as cross sections. Figure 3.10 shows a template

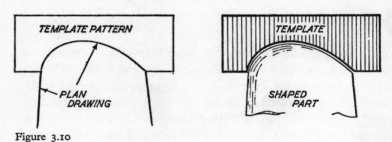

Figure 3.10

being used to check a wing tip shape. The use of a template not only ensures a correct shape, exactly matching the original plan, but also that the shape of the other tip is identical.

The importance of using templates to check cross section shapes and critical outline shapes should never be overlooked in solid scale modelling.

Constructional plans

In the case of built-up models the outline plan is only a starting point. It is usual for parts to be built flat over the plan as far as possible – see Chapter 11. This means redrawing separate plans for the wings, fuselage, tailplane and fin in the case of aircraft models, spread out so that they do not interfere with one another (figure 3.11). The necessary constructional details for building

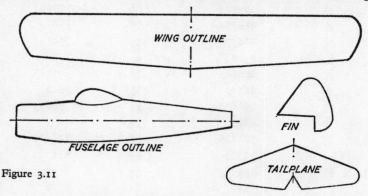

Figure 3.11

over are then added to these outline shapes, which then become working plans for the components involved.

Obviously considerably more work is involved here. In fact, after preparing the outline plan the whole project then has to be worked out as a built-up model design, which calls for experience in deciding the best type of structure to use, wood sizes required, the positioning of individual members, and so on. This experience is best obtained in building several models from published plans (or kits) first. Similar construction can then be adapted to other outline designs.

Table 3: Inch Fractions as Decimals

Fraction	Decimal Equiv.	Fraction	Decimal Equiv.
$\frac{1}{64}$	.015625	$\frac{33}{64}$	.515625
$\frac{1}{32}$	.03125	$\frac{17}{32}$	.53125
$\frac{3}{64}$	.046875	$\frac{35}{64}$	.546875
$\frac{1}{16}$	.0625	$\frac{9}{16}$	.5625
$\frac{5}{64}$	.078125	$\frac{37}{64}$	.578125
$\frac{3}{32}$	.09375	$\frac{19}{32}$	.59375
$\frac{7}{64}$	.109375	$\frac{39}{64}$	.609375
$\frac{1}{8}$	.1250	$\frac{5}{8}$	.6250
$\frac{9}{64}$	.140625	$\frac{41}{64}$	.640625
$\frac{5}{32}$	.15625	$\frac{21}{32}$	.65625
$\frac{11}{64}$	.171875	$\frac{43}{64}$	.571875
$\frac{3}{16}$	.1875	$\frac{11}{16}$	.6875
$\frac{13}{64}$	.203125	$\frac{45}{64}$	.703125
$\frac{7}{32}$	.21875	$\frac{23}{32}$	.71875
$\frac{15}{64}$	.234375	$\frac{47}{64}$	.734375
$\frac{1}{4}$	.2500	$\frac{7}{8}$	.7500
$\frac{17}{64}$	.265625	$\frac{49}{64}$	.765625
$\frac{9}{32}$	.28125	$\frac{25}{32}$	.78125
$\frac{19}{64}$	.296875	$\frac{51}{64}$	.796875
$\frac{5}{16}$	.3125	$\frac{13}{16}$	.8125
$\frac{21}{64}$	.328125	$\frac{53}{64}$	.828125
$\frac{11}{32}$	.34375	$\frac{27}{32}$	.84375
$\frac{23}{64}$	.359375	$\frac{55}{64}$	.859375
$\frac{3}{8}$	.3750	$\frac{7}{8}$	.8750
$\frac{25}{64}$	.390625	$\frac{57}{64}$	.890625
$\frac{13}{32}$	.40625	$\frac{29}{32}$	.90625
$\frac{27}{64}$	.421875	$\frac{59}{64}$	.92185
$\frac{7}{16}$	.4375	$\frac{15}{16}$	.9375
$\frac{29}{64}$	.453125	$\frac{61}{64}$	.953125
$\frac{15}{32}$	.46875	$\frac{31}{32}$	.96875
$\frac{31}{64}$	.484375	$\frac{63}{64}$	.984375
$\frac{1}{2}$	.5000	1	1.000

This table will be found particularly useful when working with decimal conversion factors for scaling up drawings

Table 4: Decimal Fractions of a Foot

FRAC-TIONS	WHOLE INCHES											
	0	1	2	3	4	5	6	7	8	9	10	11
—	—	·083	·167	·250	·333	·417	·500	·583	·667	·750	·833	·917
$\frac{1}{16}$	·005	·089	·172	·255	·339	·422	·505	·589	·672	·755	·839	·922
$\frac{1}{8}$	·010	·094	·177	·260	·344	·427	·510	·593	·677	·760	·844	·927
$\frac{3}{16}$	·016	·099	·183	·266	·349	·432	·516	·599	·682	·766	·849	·932
$\frac{1}{4}$	·021	·104	·188	·271	·354	·438	·521	·604	·688	·771	·854	·938
$\frac{5}{16}$	·026	·109	·193	·276	·359	·443	·526	·609	·693	·776	·859	·943
$\frac{3}{8}$	·031	·115	·198	·281	·365	·448	·531	·615	·698	·781	·865	·948
$\frac{7}{16}$	·036	·120	·203	·286	·370	·453	·536	·620	·703	·786	·870	·953
$\frac{1}{2}$	·042	·125	·208	·292	·375	·458	·542	·625	·708	·792	·875	·958
$\frac{9}{16}$	·047	·130	·214	·297	·380	·464	·547	·630	·714	·797	·880	·963
$\frac{5}{8}$	·052	·135	·219	·302	·385	·469	·552	·635	·719	·802	·885	·969
$\frac{11}{16}$	·057	·141	·224	·307	·391	·474	·557	·641	·724	·807	·891	·974
$\frac{3}{4}$	·063	·146	·229	·313	·396	·479	·563	·646	·729	·813	·896	·979
$\frac{13}{16}$	·068	·151	·234	·318	·401	·484	·568	·651	·734	·818	·901	·984
$\frac{7}{8}$	·073	·156	·240	·323	·406	·490	·573	·656	·740	·823	·906	·990
$\frac{15}{16}$	·078	·161	·245	·378	·411	·495	·578	·661	·745	·828	·911	·995

This table will be found particularly useful for metric conversions of mixed feet and inch units; and also for determining the inch and inch fraction equivalent of conversions rendered in feet and decimal fractions of a foot.

4 Solid Model Aircraft

The term 'solid' refers to a model which is carved from solid blocks of wood. A wood carving is a typical example of a 'solid' model, in this case carved from a single block of wood. However, this treatment would be wasteful of material and time applied to many scale model subjects, and so solid scale models are more usually carved from separate pieces of wood, subsequently joined together to complete the model. Thus a twin-engined aircraft, for example, would be carved from six separate pieces, as shown in figure 4.1. This not only simplifies construction but it also enables the grain of the wood to be selected to run in the best direction in each piece.

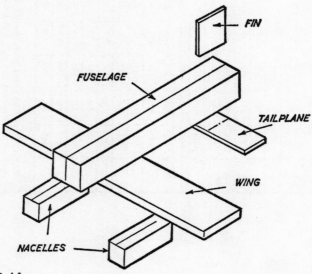

Figure 4.1

Kits for solid scale model aircraft first appeared in the early 1930s. They were immensely popular and formed the major part of model aircraft kit productions right through until the end of World War II, when some hundreds of different kits of this type were on sale in this country alone. All sorts of woods were used, particularly during the war years when balsa was in short supply, but balsa was the primary choice because of the ease with which it can be carved, especially with small scale subjects. 1/72nd scale has been the main standard for solid model aircraft since they first appeared, and it needs a skilled craftsman to produce accurate carved components to this scale in hard woods, whereas only a little practice is needed to produce the same shapes in balsa, and in a fraction of the time.

The solid scale model was virtually 'killed' by the introduction of plastic kits shortly after World War II. Plastic mouldings can reproduce finer detail than can be achieved on wood carvings, and all components can be supplied as finished shapes, self-coloured if necessary. The solid modeller's interest is mainly in collection, and the plastic kit provides a short-cut answer. No model *building* is involved − just a matter of *assembly*. Also the quality of the scale model assembled from the plastic kit is far higher than the standard likely to be achieved by any ordinary modeller starting from scratch, because both the original pattern and the dies for making the plastic kit moulds have been produced by highly skilled craftsmen.

The plastic kit model has, therefore, assumed a rightful place in meeting a collector's needs. It has also taken the craftsmanship out of scale modelling, so that the old art of solid modelling has largely died out. Not entirely, however, for there are still people who find constructing models just as satisfying as collecting them, or even more so because each model built from scratch is an example of personal skill and ability. Moreover, knowing how to build a solid scale model from scratch means that one can add to a collection a subject which is not available as a plastic kit, or as a kit in the particular scale required.

Basic technique

The basic technique is the same for the construction of a solid scale model of any type of aircraft. The subject is broken down into individual components, which are treated separately for shaping. In fact, two groups of components are involved – the *basic group* which comprises the main components such as wings, fuselage, tailplane and fin (and engine nacelles in the case of multi-engined aircraft); and the *detail group* which comprises all smaller items which are best made separately, and fitted to the basic group when these main components have been assembled.

The first thing necessary is to obtain a plan (or draw one up) to the required scale. All the shapes required for the basic group can then be taken directly off this plan. Some thought is then necessary to decided how the basic group components are to be joined, as this will affect their shape to some extent.

The main joint is usually between the wing and fuselage. Figure 4.2 shows three possible ways of making this joint. With

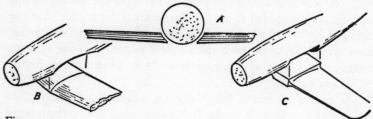

Figure 4.2

both A and B the shaping of the two components to make a good joint will be very tricky. Also making the wing in two halves to be joined to the side of the fuselage will produce a weak assembly. Both A and B, therefore, are poor. It is far better if the centre piece of the wing is left square, as in C, to fit into a corresponding 'square' cut out in the fuselage. Not only will this type of joint be easier to make, but it will be strong.

For a low wing monoplane, therefore, plan to slot the wing into the bottom of the fuselage (figure 4.3). For a high wing

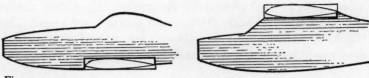

Figure 4.3

monoplane the wing can usually rest in a cut-out on top of the fuselage. In the case of a mid-wing layout, a deeper slot is required, either cut from the top or bottom, depending on which produces the least depth of cut-out (figure 4.4).

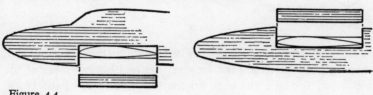

Figure 4.4

A suitable fixing for the *tailplane* can be decided in a similar manner. Again the tailplane should be made in one piece for accuracy and ease of assembly. Usually it can be accommodated in a slot cut in the top or bottom of the fuselage (figure 4.5). If in

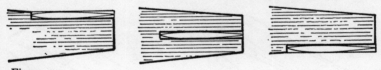

Figure 4.5

a mid position, it can be fitted into a slot cut in the end of the fuselage.

Having decided the method of joining the components comprising the basic group, the shaping of the individual components can be considered separately.

Fuselage

Hard balsa is preferred for this component. First a block of balsa is cut to slightly oversize dimensions, i.e., slightly deeper and wider than the scale fuselage size but to exact length. This should be marked with a centreline on the top and bottom, and a datum line on each side (figure 4.6).

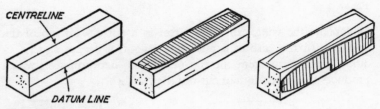

CENTRELINE

DATUM LINE

Figure 4.6

Using a template, tracing, or whatever method is preferred, mark out the fuselage plan view on top and bottom faces of the block and the side elevation on the two side faces of the block, aligning over the centrelines and datum lines respectively. Next mark on the cut out positions for the wings and tailplane. This completes marking out the block.

The next step is to turn this block into a blank. Use a saw to cut to the side elevation shape (figure 4.7). Make sure that the

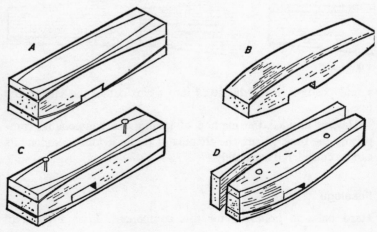

A

B

C

D

Figure 4.7

cut is square, which is where marking the shape on both sides of the block will be a help.

Form the cut outs for the wing and tailplane. Then pin back the two pieces originally removed and saw the block to plan shape. Remove the original pieces and you are left with a squared up fuselage blank ready for carving.

Carving should proceed in careful stages. Work from the centre of the blank towards each end, taking only small cuts at a time until the whole blank is reduced to rough shape. At this stage you will need templates to check the section (see Chapter 3). Offer up templates at various positions on each side and continue carving until each template nearly fits (figure 4.8). Final shaping

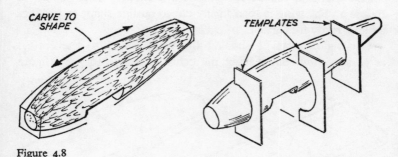

Figure 4.8

down to finished size should then be done with fine glasspaper. This will remove any knife marks, so by the time the fuselage is reduced to its proper section the surface will be smooth.

Wings

Medium block should be suitable for the wings. Cut the block slightly oversize with sufficient depth to allow for any dihedral on the wings – (figure 4.9). Mark the dihedral and wing taper on both front and back of the block. Use a half template to mark out the wing outline shape on top of the block. This will ensure that each wing outline is exactly the same. Finally mark on the 'square' centre portion of the wing where it fits into the fuselage cut out.

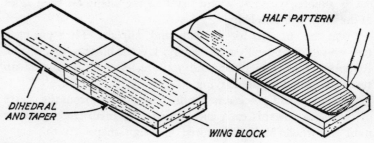

Figure 4.9

The wing block should be cut to taper and dihedral first (figure 4.10). If this removes the top markings, these should be redrawn. The wing is then finally cut to outline shape to produce a blank ready for carving.

Carving consists of shaping the wing halves to the correct *aerofoil section*, but leaving the centre portion 'square' (figure

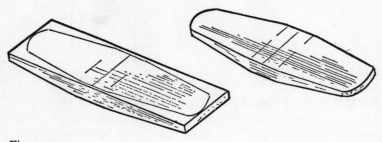

Figure 4.10

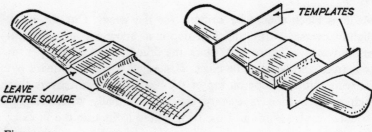

Figure 4.11

4.11). Again templates must be used to check this section, and final finishing done by sanding so as not to leave any knife marks on the surface. Be sure to work the trailing edge down to a sharp and *straight* line. Drawing this line on the edge of the blank before starting carving will help.

Swept wings

Swept wings can be a bit of a problem, especially if they are long and narrow. If possible they should be carved from a single piece, although this may mean wasting quite a bit of balsa. On larger models it may be better to build the wing blank up from separate pieces, as shown in figure 4.12. A dowel can be used to

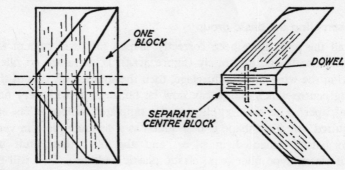

Figure 4.12

strengthen the centre joint, but must come within the outline of the aerofoil section.

Separate construction for the wing blank may also be the simplest solution where wings have a lot of dihedral. It may not be possible to incorporate any dowel reinforcement, in which case the joint to the centre piece should be double-cemented.

Tail parts

The tailplane and fin can be cut from sheet balsa of suitable thickness. After cutting to outline shape, mark the centreline right round the edge of each piece and then finish to aerofoil section by sanding only. Note that in the case of the tailplane the centre is left 'square' again to fit into the fuselage slot (figure 4.13).

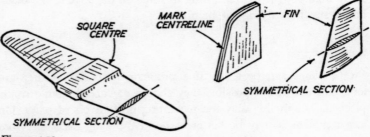

Figure 4.13

Assembling the basic group

If all the parts have been correctly shaped they will cement together neatly and accurately (figure 4.14). If there are no fillets fairing the wing into the fuselage, then the squared off part of the wing centre which shows can now be finished off with very fine sandpaper. The same applies to the tailplane. Where fillets are required, the fillet shape is best added as a separate piece in very thin balsa, cemented in place, and the fillet then built up with elastic type filler (e.g., elastic plastic padding). This will be easy to sand down to shape to produce a final fillet blending

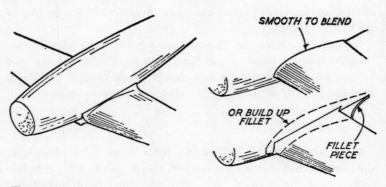

Figure 4.14

properly with the lines of the fuselage. Do not use plastic wood or hard-setting body fillers for this job.

Painting the basic group

At this stage the model should be treated with grain filler, sanded down absolutely smooth all over and finish painted. Detail markkings, etc., can be scored on after filling and before final painting.

The detail group

Completing the model is then very much like plastic model assembly, adding the detail parts one by one to the basic group. The only difference is that these detail parts will have to be made from suitable materials. Harder material than balsa is preferred for small, fragile parts. You can, in fact, often use parts from a plastic kit, such as propellers, wheels, undercarriage parts, etc. Undercarriages are best left off solid models if possible, as they are difficult to duplicate neatly. With patience and care, however, all necessary small parts can be carved from scraps of hardwood or bamboo, or bent from thin wire, etc.

Canopies are another problem. The simple way with solid models is to carve the canopy in with the fuselage shape, or add it to the basic group as a separate piece. Window areas are then painted matt black and frame lines picked out in silver paint or coloured dope, as appropriate, using a ruling pen. This can give quite a realistic appearance (figure 4.15). Again, however, it may be possible to fit a transparent canopy from a plastic kit, or even make a suitable moulding from acetate sheet over a balsa shape. Tackling the detail parts, in fact, is largely a matter of ingenuity and how far you are prepared to go in using plastic kit parts, or copying plastic kit parts in other materials. A plastic kit itself is a very good guide as to what the finished detail parts should look like.

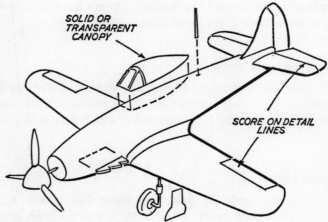

Figure 4.15

Nacelles

Nacelles on multi-engined models can be a bit of a problem to fit to wings. The nacelle block *can* be shaped to fit accurately over the aerofoil section of the wing (figure 4.16), but this can be quite tricky. This is probably the simplest way, though, and any gaps in the joint can be filled with elastic filler. Note that

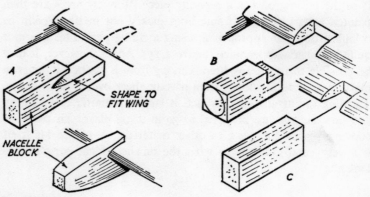

Figure 4.16

the nacelle should be shaped to fit the wing whilst still in the block stage. It is then treated like a fuselage for cutting to blank shape and then carving to final shape.

Alternative treatments for nacelles are shown in diagrams B and C. These may be more appropriate in particular cases. The actual carving of nacelles is the same as for fuselages.

5 Silhouette Models

Silhouette construction is a quick and simple method of producing solid scale models which are accurate in shape and form, but lack detail. They are intended as *recognition* models rather than display models and are normally painted matt black with no detail or markings added. This type of construction is normally applied to aircraft models, but can be used for other subjects.

The basis of a silhouette model is a series of outline shapes cut from sheet balsa and assembled in the form of a simple 'silhouette' or three-dimensional model lacking thickness, as shown in figure 5.1. Cutting out these parts is simple. The fuselage, wing and tail shapes are transferred directly to balsa sheet and cut out accurately. Wing and tail are notched into the fuselage, and all parts are glued together with balsa cement.

Patterns are now made up of the thickness shapes. Thus the

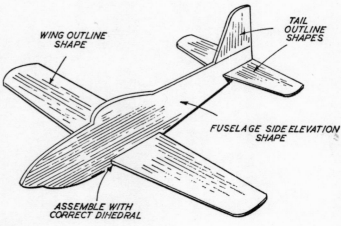

Figure 5.1

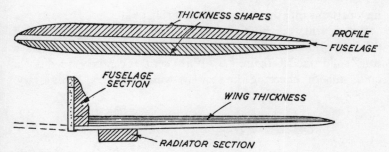

THICKNESS SHAPES

PROFILE
FUSELAGE

FUSELAGE
SECTION

WING THICKNESS

RADIATOR SECTION

Figure 5.2

fuselage half thickness is represented by a pattern cut as shown in figure 5.2, with a suitable allowance for the thickness of the sheet from which the silhouette fuselage was cut. The wing thickness pattern is plotted in a similar way. Additional patterns may also be required for protuberances, such as a radiator slung under the wing.

These patterns are then cemented to the basic silhouette model, as shown in figure 5.3. The result is a model which is both accurate in outline, and correct as regards 'thickness' or solidity when viewed from a distance. The overall effect is much better if the whole model is painted matt black as this blends the thick-

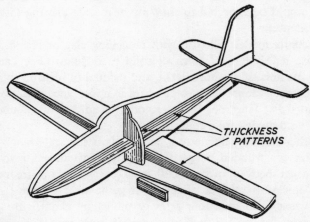

THICKNESS
PATTERNS

Figure 5.3

ness patterns into the mass of the main shapes.

Better still, the built-up pattern can be left unpainted and filled in with modelling clay or plastic padding to complete a true 'solid' model (figure 5.4). When set this can be sanded down quite smooth, checking the sections with templates, if necessary.

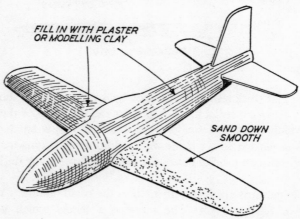

FILL IN WITH PLASTER OR MODELLING CLAY

SAND DOWN SMOOTH

Figure 5.4

Once again the completed model should be painted matt black all over, with no attempt to add detail other than external detail which would be expected to show up at a scale viewing distance – see Chapter 2.

Silhouette models filled in with modelling clay or plastic padding are a 'short cut' form of solid modelling. They can, of course, be finished in more detail, and painted in realistic colours, although they cannot hope to compare in appearance with normal solid models. They do, however, offer a quick way of making background models for a collection.

Another use for silhouette type models is for scale mock-ups, with the construction adapted to the type of subject involved. Thus a car body or a boat hull mock-up would require rather more 'thickness' shapes added as a guide to a proper 'solid' shape when filled in with plaster or modelling clay (figure 5.5).

A particular use for such mock-ups in scale modelling is as a

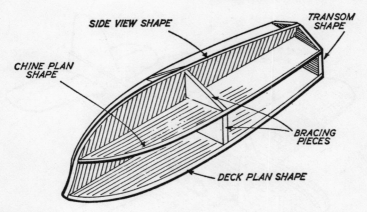

Figure 5.5

former or plug for covering with glass fibre to produce a female mould. Once this mould has been made further glass fibre mouldings or body shells can be taken off it. This is an effective way of producing a series of identical car body shells, or boat hulls. The use of balsa for constructing the basic shapes and formers of the mock-up considerably simplifies the construction of the plug.

Profile models

A further variation of silhouette-type construction is seen in the *profile* model, a type of control line model aircraft. This has scale fuselage, wing and tail shapes, but all these parts are cut from sheet balsa. Only the wing will have any shaping to reduce the thickness necessary for strength and rigidity to an efficient aerofoil section for flying (figure 5.6).

The profile model is semi-scale rather than scale, but with much of the appearance of a scale model in flight. This is helped by mounting the engine sideways so that a realistic nose profile is maintained. The whole model is also usually finished in suitable colours with scale markings and detail.

The advantages of a profile model are that it is quick and simple to make. The outline shapes have only to be plotted on to sheet balsa and cut out. The fuselage nose is then reinforced

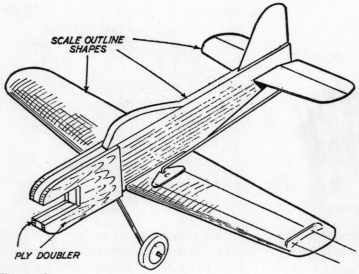

Figure 5.6

with ply doublers on each side to carry the engine. The wing is carved and sanded to aerofoil section, just like a solid model (Chapter 4) and the control system is mounted externally, with the bellcrank pivoted to the wing close to the fuselage.

The main limitation is the size of model which can be built successfully as a flying model with all sheet balsa construction. Strength and weight considerations generally limit the maximum fuselage length or wingspan to about 30 inches. The fuselage rather than the wing is likely to be the weak member for a profile control line model, as size is increased. A solution in this case is to build up the fuselage from two sheet sides with a narrow but deep top and bottom section to produce a hollow box section.

The profile type model is essentially designed as a functional or working model. Although it is mostly used for control line aircraft it can equally well be applied to small free flight models. Size in such cases is usually restricted to about 24 inches wingspan maximum, for light weight is more important on a free flight model than a control line model.

Where the free flight profile model is designed for rubber power, the rubber motor is taken through a cut out portion of the profile fuselage (figure 5.7). A rubber-powered model aeroplane

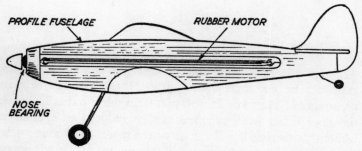

PROFILE FUSELAGE   RUBBER MOTOR

NOSE
BEARING

Figure 5.7

requires an over-scale propeller, with a correspondingly longer undercarriage to suit. Tail surface areas also have to be increased substantially above scale proportions, also the wing dihedral. The resulting model is thus far from true in outline shape and cannot be classed as anything but a simple semi-scale model.

6 Waterline Ship Models

Accurate waterline scale ship models are easy to make since they can be cut and assembled in 'layers', which simplifies construction. The most difficult part is finishing in detail, although the finer detail work required can be reduced to a minimum without destroying the character of the model. Too much detail, and particularly out-of-scale detail (usually too coarse or 'heavy') will detract from, rather than add to, the final appearance of the model.

Starting point once again must be a scale drawing of the ship it is intended to model, showing a side view and plan view. It will be a great help if photographs or magazine illustrations of the ship are also available for reference. These will be invaluable in helping to decide what actual shapes should be, and particularly detail shapes, which are not often clear on drawings, and sometimes not included on them at all.

The hull

The hull is the main part and should be constructed first. Study the side view drawing and decide how the main hull shape can most conveniently be divided up into 'block' shapes. Quite often this will break down into one large black for the main part of the hull, on which can be superimposed two or more smaller, shallower blocks – e.g. see figure 6.1.

If the deck line has curvature running from fore to aft, or sheer, then it may be simpler to add two or three thin layers to the basic hull block, as shown in figure 6.2, rather than attempt to cut this curved line out from the main block. This will produce both quicker and more accurate results, it being

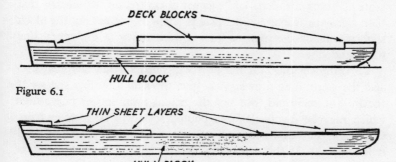

Figure 6.1

Figure 6.2

necessary only to glue these thin layers to the main block, wait for them to set and then blend down into a smooth sheerline curve by sanding, making sure that the joint lines do not show. If the joint lines do show, however carefully you do sand down, then a simple solution is to cut a pattern in thin card which will fit right over the deck as an additional layer. Once cut to an exact matching shape this should be prepainted before gluing down to the hull block.

Having decided on a suitable depth for the main hull block, cut out a suitable block of hard balsa and mark on the plan the shape of the hull at deck level (figure 6.3). The use of a half tem-

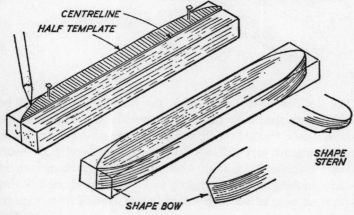

Figure 6.3

plate is recommended, laid against a centreline, to ensure that both sides are absolutely identical in shape. Then cut out the block slightly outside the marked lines. Finish down to the actual line with sandpaper.

To complete the hull the bow will need further shaping, and also the stern. The drawing will give the actual outline shapes of the hull at each end, but not the actual rounding or curvatures which may be involved. Here photographs will be a great help. Carve and sand down the hull ends to the required shape, or until it looks right. If the top of the rudder shows above the water-line at the stern, do not attempt to carve this shape in with the hull but cut off vertically. The top of the rudder can then be cut from a separate thin piece of balsa sheet and cemented on later.

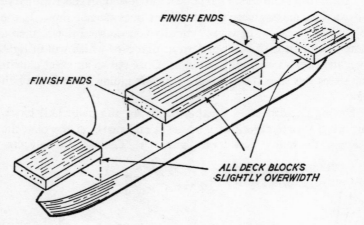

FINISH ENDS

FINISH ENDS

ALL DECK BLOCKS
SLIGHTLY OVERWIDTH

Figure 6.4

The smaller blocks completing the hull shape can then be added. These should be cut slightly oversize in width. Also the ends should be finished off smooth and square before cementing in place. It will be very difficult to work on these end grain areas and get them really smooth when the blocks are cemented in position. Making the blocks slightly wider than the actual hull also makes it easier to blend them smoothly into the hull sides, with no joint showing.

All these smaller blocks are cut as 'square' pieces. Once set in position the blocks at the bow and stern can be carved down to rough shape and finally finished off with sandpaper. Again this is the best method of blending these smaller blocks into the main hull block shape. The bow block in particular may have quite a curvature on it to blend into the flare of the main hull, which will be more obvious from photographs than from a drawing.

At this stage the hull may be treated with sanding sealer and painted, bearing in mind that the deck finish will always be matt and the hull sides also usually matt, but sometimes glossy on passenger liners. Nothing looks worse than the wrong type of finish on a scale model – a glossy colour where it should be matt.

Further deck layers may now have to be added, one by one. Figure 6.5, for example, shows the build-up of decks on a modern

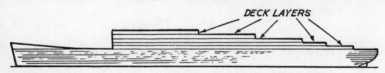

Figure 6.5

liner, each deck cut as a separate layer and cemented in place. The actual length and shape required for each piece can readily be determined from the plan view drawing. Edges should be sealed and sanded smooth and square before cementing in place, as with the small hull blocks.

An important point to bear in mind when building up deck layers is the *scale* of the model. Ships' decks are usually about 8 feet high, so the thickness of each layer should correspond to this scale height. This may mean sanding down standard thicknesses of balsa sheet. For example, a 1/1000th scale model would require deck layers 8/1000ths of a foot or approximately 1/10th of an inch thick. In this case 3/32 inch thick sheet would be about right. For a 1/2000th scale model, however, the deck thickness required would be 1/20th of an inch thick at the most, which would mean using 1/16 inch sheet and reducing its thickness slightly by sanding. See also Table 5 p 67.

An alternative method of obtaining a really neat finish to deck layers is shown in figure 6.6. Once built up in place, the whole superstructure is then covered with a piece of paper, carefully scored and bent to fit over the 'steps'. This paper covering can be prepainted, usually in white, before it is glued in place. It will provide a much neater surface, with squarer edges, than the original balsa layers.

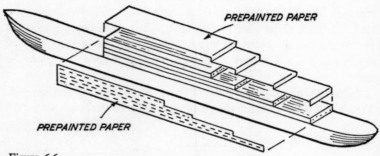

PREPAINTED PAPER

PREPAINTED PAPER

Figure 6.6

The same treatment can be applied to the sides of the built-up decking. In this case it may be possible to duplicate portholes or windows by punching a neat line of holes in the paper, using a piece of small metal tube filed to a cutting edge. If the balsa layers are then painted matt black before the paper covering is applied, the resulting appearance can be quite realistic. The paper covering should be prepainted again before finally gluing in place. PVA or white glue is usually the most suitable adhesive for fixing paper coverings of this type.

On a larger model it will be necessary to show an open deck outside the 'cabin' layers rather than a solid side to the superstructure. In this case the decks can be formed from pieces of very thin but stiff card, sandwiched between the balsa layers, as shown in figure 6.7. Vertical fill-in sections can then be added, as necessary, cut from very thin balsa sheet.

The bridge area will need further treatment and building up. Balsa 'layer' construction can be used, together with thin card for 'open' deck areas or wings to the bridge. Glazed areas can

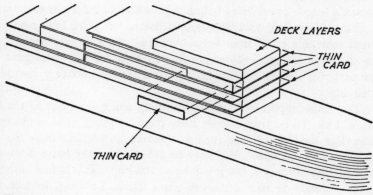

Figure 6.7

be represented by small pieces of acetate sheet stuck between the open decks, with divisions between windows formed by gluing in tiny slivers of bamboo, or perhaps short lengths of cotton. If a *water soluble* glue is used for such attachments, surplus glue can be removed with a damp brush once the original pieces have set in position.

Funnels can be a bit of a problem. Many modern steamship funnels have a rounded, closed top, when the required shape can easily be carved from balsa, or two or three small balsa blocks cemented together. However, solid construction does not look realistic for a funnel which is open at the top. In this case the funnel shape is best carved from block balsa, finished by sanding to slightly undersize. This is then rubbed over with a candle and several layers of gumstrip wound round it. When dry, the gumstrip is removed from the balsa, cutting away the balsa to free the funnel if necessary. This hollow gumstrip funnel can then be trimmed to size and sanded down smooth. It should then be painted before cementing in place.

The amount of further detail to be added then depends largely on the size of the model. To ensure a scale appearance, masts need to be quite thin, so balsa is unsuitable. Instead, shape these from matchsticks or thin bamboo split down to a suitable size. Crosstrees are best made from thin slivers of bamboo, cut to suitable length and secured with a minute blob of balsa cement.

Tiny parts such as lifeboats, ventilators, etc., are best made from materials other than balsa. Although balsa is easy enough to shape, it is practically impossible to hold a small balsa part properly for sealing and sanding down perfectly smooth prior to painting.

The same applies to bulwarks running along the edge of the main deck. To be true to scale these must be paper thin on most waterline models, so thin card is a better proposition than the thinnest of balsa sheet. You may be able to sand the balsa down to a suitable thickness, but it will be almost impossible to seal both sides properly to take a smooth paint finish. Painting, in fact, is one of the trickiest parts when it comes to completing the detail.

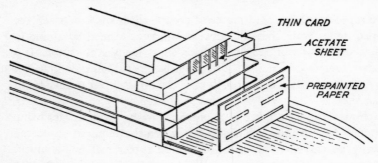

Figure 6.8

As far as possible all detail parts should be prepainted before they are fitted, unless they are the same colour as the part to which they are attached.

Davits can be formed from fuse wire. This can be hammered to produce a flat rather than a round section, once the davit shape has been bent. Fuse wire may also be used for stanchions, or alternatively thin slivers of bamboo. The use of balsa is best restricted to the main 'sandwich' construction on waterline model ships, except for simple 'square' shapes which can be furnished by covering with prepainted paper.

The amount of detail which is to be added to complete the model is largely a matter of individual preference and ingenuity in making the various fittings and parts. The main thing is that that all detail should look right, and in scale, never overdone, for the size of the model.

Full depth ship models

Exactly the same type of 'layer' construction can, of course, be used for making scale model ships with a full hull depth. In this case the main hull block is made deeper, to accommodate the full depth side elevation. After shaping to plan view, the hull block is then carved down to the proper sections along its length. These sections can be checked with templates, as carving proceeds. If the hull has a keel piece extending below the bottom of the hull, this should be added later as a separate glued-on strip.

Table 5: Scale Thicknesses for Deck Layers

Scale	Scale thickness (inch)	Nearest standard balsa sheet (inch size)
$\frac{1}{96}$	1	1
$\frac{1}{100}$	1	1
$\frac{1}{200}$	$\frac{1}{2}$	$\frac{1}{2}$
$\frac{1}{400}$	$\frac{1}{4}$	$\frac{1}{4}$
$\frac{1}{500}$	$\frac{1}{5}$	$\frac{3}{16}$
$\frac{1}{600}$	$\frac{1}{6}$	$\frac{1}{8}$
$\frac{1}{1000}$	$\frac{1}{10}$	$\frac{3}{32}$
$\frac{1}{2000}$	$\frac{1}{20}$	$\frac{1}{16}$
$\frac{1}{3000}$	$\frac{1}{80}$	$\frac{1}{32}$
$\frac{1}{4000}$	$\frac{1}{40}$	$\frac{1}{32}$

7   Ships in Bottles

Waterline ship models are essentially display models or collector's items. They are best kept in cabinets or individual display cases where they cannot collect dust. An interesting alternative is building up such a model inside a bottle -- the obvious question to anyone seeing the finished job being, ' How on earth did the ship get inside the bottle?' You will have seen examples yourself from time to time and probably wondered the same thing.

Ships in bottles are models built for effect. They are seldom true scale models, but realistic enough to look like a scale model or miniature ship. They are thought out with effect in mind. Obviously a long, slender model such as a destroyer which is slim enough to be passed through the neck of the bottle complete is not going to excite anything like the same interest as a ship in a bottle which can only have got there by having been built up piece by piece *inside* the bottle. That is the effect required -- making the job look impossible. It is not true scale modelling, but it is an interesting and challenging subject for modellers who like the unusual.

There are a number of different techniques for building ships in bottles -- in fact, whole books have been written about this particular subject. Only simple techniques will be described here. Other ideas and more complicated methods of treatment will occur to individual modellers after their first attempts.

One thing is obvious for a start. No object can be got inside the bottle if it is larger than the opening of the neck. This determines the largest solid *sections* which can be got into the bottle. Larger sections will have to be split and reassembled inside the bottle, although there is the further possibility of passing some large parts through the neck by folding them up, or curving them.

It is also obvious that the whole of the model will have to be painted before it is introduced into the bottle.

The first requirement is a good working base inside the bottle to which the model can be secured. This will ensure that the model can be worked on as necessary inside the bottle, and will also stop the finished model from moving around and possibly

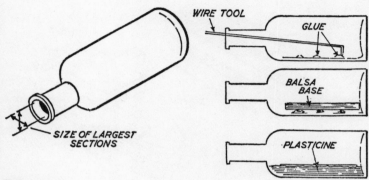

Figure 7.1

damaging itself. Figure 7.1 shows how to assemble the base inside the bottle.

Make a simple tool from a piece of galvanized iron wire, as shown, to put a number of blobs of *epoxy* adhesive in line on the inside of the glass. Cut a piece of balsa strip to suitable length, pass through the neck of the bottle and position over the adhesive blobs, using the same tool, and press down firmly. This will now need leaving for about twenty-four hours for the adhesive to set hard, but the process can be speeded up by putting the bottle in a warm place. Once the adhesive has set the balsa strip will be securely and permanently bonded to the inside of the bottle.

A suitable 'sea' now needs adding, built up around each side of the strip, but leaving the top uncovered. This can be made from sea-green-coloured plasticine, introduced bit by bit through the neck of the bottle and worked down flat. When the right level of 'sea' has been built up, the surface can be worked over with the wire tool to form waves. The same tool, dipped in white paint, can be used to paint crests on some of the waves, if desired.

Construction of the model follows the same technique as that for waterline scale models (Chapter 6), except that the hull block is made up from as many separate sections as are necessary for each to pass through the neck of the bottle (figure 7.2). These

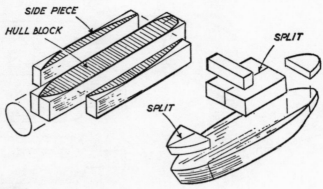

Figure 7.2

separate pieces should be tack-glued together lightly – i.e., just glued at one or two spots – and shaped in the normal way. Then separate into pieces again.

Deck and superstructure layers are then built up, but not glued to the hull block. Simply lay them in position. Decided how these may have to be split to pass through the neck of the bottle. The bridge and funnel(s) can be regarded as separate items, again simply laid in position, not glued. You should then have a collection of pieces, all of which will pass through the neck of the bottle.

Now examine the breakdown of the pieces to see which joints will show. It will be impossible to make neat glued joints when assembling the pieces inside the bottle, and so these need to be hidden. This can be done with paper layers cut to an exact shape. Since these paper shapes will be wider than the neck of the bottle they will have to be bent into a curve to pass through the neck of the bottle. This means that they will all have to be straight

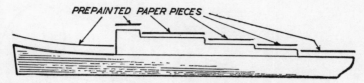

PREPAINTED PAPER PIECES

Figure 7.3

pieces (figures 7.3). They cannot be bent into a stepped shape, unless this is small enough to manoeuvre through the bottle neck sideways.

All the individual pieces of the model should now be painted including the paper coverings. The hull blocks should be painted around the inside surface of the joints as well, as this will help to hide the joint when finally assembled. Reassemble the model when dry to check that there are no unpainted areas which show. If masts are to be fitted, pierce holes at the mast positions.

Using the wire tool, transfer balsa cement to the top of the base piece inside the bottle and cover this surface generously. Using two similar tools of clean wire, pass the centre hull block through the neck and position over the base, pressing down firmly (figure 7.4). Leave to set. You now have a rigid assembly around which the rest of the model can be assembled.

The side blocks to complete the hull should be coated with balsa cement on the joint side. They can then be carried into the

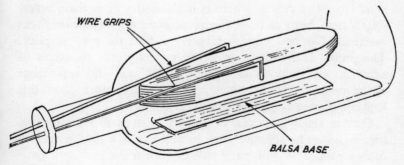

WIRE GRIPS

BALSA BASE

Figure 7.4

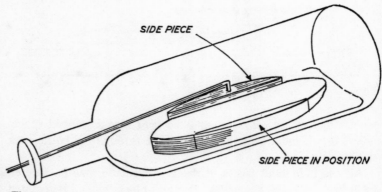

SIDE PIECE

SIDE PIECE IN POSITION

Figure 7.5

bottle on a length of wire one at a time, as shown in figure 7.5 and pressed in place with the same tool. The paper covering pieces follow, this time coated with photographic paste or ordinary gum. This will allow them to be 'shuffled' into position as necessary, when they can be smoothed out flat with the wire tool to take out any curl remaining from their passage through the bottle neck.

All the remaining pieces are then built up, one by one, in the same fashion, except that the gluing technique may vary. Where possible, apply glue to the part of the model already built up so that the new part can be passed in 'dry' and laid in place. This will eliminate any possibility of smearing the other surfaces with glue. Use balsa cement where possible as this gives the quickest setting time, but PVA or photographic paste will be best for paper coverings. Use only enough adhesive to hold the parts in place. The joints do not have to be very strong and an excess of adhesive, especially balsa cement, could ruin the appearance of the model if squeezed out of a joint. If in any doubt about this happening, use PVA glue instead of balsa cement.

Further small parts can be carried in stuck to the wire tool (figure 7.6). The adhesive used in this case is a tiny amount of rubber gum. This will easily pull free when the part is in position, and any rubber gum which remains on the part can be

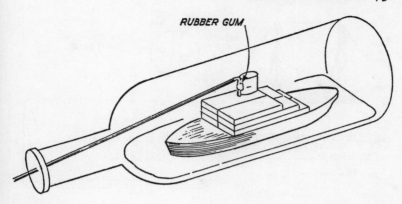

RUBBER GUM

Figure 7.6

rubbed off with a wire tool when the part has set firmly in position.

All the necessary tool shapes for handling the various parts to be assembled inside the bottle, as well as for spreading adhesive on the assembly, can be bent from stiff wire. You may, however, find other simple tools which are even more useful. A long hat pin, for example, is very useful for carrying small balsa parts; and so are long narrow tweezers.

Full rigged ships

For model sailing ships in bottles a different technique is usually employed. The hull size chosen should be small enough to pass easily through the neck of the bottle and the whole model is built complete, and fully rigged, outside the bottle. The masts are then notched at the most suitable height, so that they and the whole of the standing rigging can be folded down flat on top of the hull, with the main forestay loose to act as a 'drawstring' (figure 7.7). Once inside the bottle and with the hull glued down to its base piece, masts and rigging are erected by pulling on the forestay which is then made off taut around the end of the bowsprit.

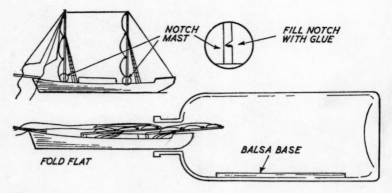

Figure 7.7

A short, deep bottle, more of a flask shape, is best for models of this type, and preferably one with a fairly generous neck size. The object is to get the largest possible size of model inside the bottle. This is not so difficult as it may seem if the model is built without sails, and with the yardarms pivoted to the mast on tiny lengths of stiff wire (figure 7.8). No rigging lines are

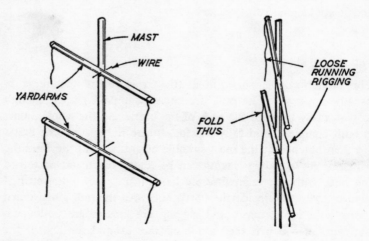

Figure 7.8

taken to the yardarms themselves which can then be turned to lie in line with the mast for folding down. In this way only a small amount of clearance above the hull is needed to get the model, with quite detailed standing rigging, through the neck of the bottle.

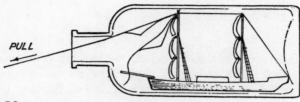

PULL

Figure 7.9

Once in position and with the masts drawn upright again, all the yardarms can be straightened and secured in a horizontal position if necessary with a tiny spot of glue applied on the end of a length of wire. Paper sails can then be cut and mounted individually on the yardarms, again with glue. Running rigging lines can be attached to the individual sails, which can be curled as necessary to pass through the bottle neck. Mounting each sail in position, and capturing and securing the running lines with a tiny blob of glue at appropriate points, can be a tricky and tedious operation, but can add greatly to the attraction of the finished model. The process can be simplified if there is sufficient clearance in the bottle neck to attach some sails to their yardarms before the model is inserted. Always try to do this, if possible, with sail positions which will be the hardest to reach once the model is inside the bottle.

Once again, of course, there are many possible variations on getting a full rigged ship inside a bottle, but the method of completing at least the main rigging, and then 'folding' the masts down is usually the simplest and most straightforward approach.

8   Solid Model Cars

Solid scale models of cars are seldom worth while constructing to a small scale. The collector's needs here are well covered by plastic and die-cast models and the detail and finish of these is superior to that which even a skilled worker can achieve with small balsa models. Solid balsa car models are, however, a worthwhile project for larger scales, where the coverage offered by plastic kits is far more limited and the cost of such kits is usually high.

For simple scale models which are to have no interior detail the whole of the car body can be carved from a single solid block of balsa, although with the majority of saloon car shapes some considerable saving in balsa is possible by using two blocks glued together (figure 8.1). Both blocks should be slightly over-size, with the required dimensions worked out from the side and end elevation dimensions of a scale drawing as shown.

A useful source of scale drawings for cars is the Test Reports featured in the motoring journals. These usually include drawings

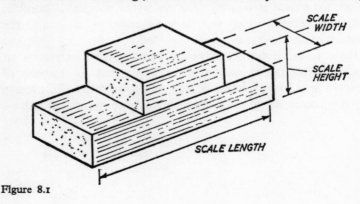

Figure 8.1

of the car to the scale of 1/20th. This is a useful scale for a solid balsa model, so these drawings could be used to provide patterns for a 1/20th scale model, or redrawn twice the size for a 1/10th scale model. In the latter case the width of block required is likely to be greater than that of standard balsa block, so two or more blocks would have to be glued up side by side. Alternatively some considerable saving in balsa may be possible by using a built-up box, assembled from block and thicker sheet (figure 8.2).

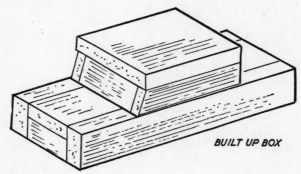

BUILT UP BOX

Figure 8.2

A template of the body side elevation should be used to mark out each side of the body block (figure 8.3). This can then be trimmed down to shape to give a square blank. At this stage the wheel arches should be marked on the sides of the blank and cut out in the form of troughs. The plan view shape can then be marked on the bottom. Trimming down to this will complete shaping of the blank, which is now ready for carving.

Carving is quite straightforward, provided cuts are always taken in a direction which avoids digging into the grain. The main cross section shape can be taken as the front view drawing shown on the plan, but intermediate cross sections are not so clear, unless you have a fully detailed model plan from which to work. They may have to be guessed, in which case the more photographs or illustrations of the car you can collect for reference the better.

Half templates should be used to check the body cross sections

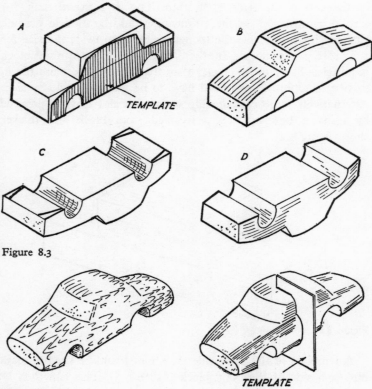

Figure 8.3

Figure 8.4

at various points (figure 8.4). Even if you are not sure of the true section at a particular point, a half section template will still be useful to check that the section you have carved is the same on each side of the body. Small discrepancies in actual section may get by on a scale model, but not a body which has a different section on one side to the other. It will look lopsided.

Where compound curves are involved, sanding sticks, or fine-medium glasspaper wrapped around a strip of hardwood, are often more effective for shaping than carving (figure 8.5). The shape of the hardwood strip backing for the glasspaper can be chosen accordingly, e.g., round dowel or half round for forming

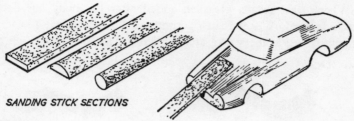

SANDING STICK SECTIONS

Figure 8.5

hollow curves. Carving should be stopped in any case before the body shape has been reduced to final size, so that the final finishing down to size can be done with fine glasspaper, leaving no knife marks showing.

Once satisfied that the body shape is correct and smooth all over, the full finishing treatment described in Chapter 2 is required – plenty of coats of sanding sealer, followed by sanding down between each coat with garnet paper. Any surface defects which show up should be filled in with body putty, or elastic padding filler. To duplicate the gloss of a full size car finish, the balsa body must be fully sealed and glass smooth all over before any finishing colours are applied.

Detail lines should be scored on to the model at this stage. Door outlines, panel lines, etc., are all prominent on full size cars and for realism these should be duplicated on the model. They are best cut with the point of a sharp knife and if necessary, further opened up with a pointed instrument. All detail lines should be added *after* sealing and sanding, and *before* finish painting.

Windows can be treated quite simply. They are left unpainted when the main body colour(s) is applied, except that this colour is allowed to overlap the window outlines very slightly. When the body colour has dried hard, window areas are then masked off with masking tape and painted matt black. This is quite effective, especially if small strips are then cut from silvered paper or thin aluminum foil, smoothed out on a sheet of glass to remove any wrinkles, and then glued in place to represent window frames.

Wheels and details are then added after the body has been finish painted. Wheels can be simply mounted on balsa blocks cemented inside the wheel arches (figure 8.6). If the rear wheel

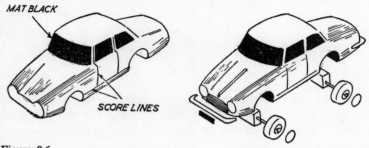

Figure 8.6

arch is faired in, a separate fairing piece should be fitted to the body after carving and smoothed down and sealed and painted *with* the body. It can then be removed for fitting the rear wheels, if necessary, and replaced.

Models of this type are not generally fully detailed, but main details such as headlamps, grille, bumpers, etc., must be fitted where appropriate. Brightwork parts which are shaped to fit can be carved from scrap balsa, then covered with aluminium foil or painted silver. Aluminium foil strips, wire mesh, aluminium wire (which can be hammered down to a flatter section) is necessary, and similar materials will all find useful application for small detail parts. Headlamps can be pieces of acetate sheet, with the lamp recess hollowed out and painted silver. Rims can be narrow strips of aluminium foil.

The detail added does not have to be exact scale. It has to look right in size and appearance – just as you would expect to see it on a full size car sufficiently far away to look the same *size* as the model.

Very much more elaborate construction is, of course, possible with balsa. To produce a model with full interior detail, for example, the original body block is first planned as a hollow box (with a separate top piece in the case of a saloon) – see figure 8.7.

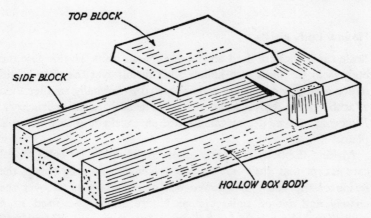

Figure 8.7

Body and top are carved and shaped separately. The top can then be mounted temporarily on suitable pillars and checked for fit. The two parts are then disassembled and finish painted. Interior detail is then added to the body before the top is finally refitted and acetate sheet windows added.

Seats and the transmission tunnel can be cut from balsa sheet and block, suitably shaped and covered with scale-looking upholstery material and carpet respectively. A suitable fixing point for the rear wheels may also have to be added under the ' trim ', if this cannot be provided by a solid rear seat. Painted card or wood veneer can be used for the instrument panel, with instruments drawn on card, cut out and stuck in position. The steering wheel is the most difficult part to make neatly with a true scale appearance. The simplest approach is to make a wire rim mounted on card spokes, and with a length of dowel for the steering column. This can be thickened at the upper end with a wrapping of gumstrip. The gear lever can be made from wire or a glass headed pin. Foot pedals can be cut from card, mounted on wire or pins. Pins and aluminium wire can be used for making door handles, etc. Fuse wire is also useful for duplicating metal edging trim.

Hollow body shells

Scale car bodies are used on slot-car chassis units. In this case the body is in the form of a hollow shell fitting over the chassis and motor and gear unit. The scale involved is normally smaller than 1/20th, but a balsa scale model is usually quite satisfactory. Motoring and model magazines are an excellent source of scale plans.

Making the body is exactly as described above for solid model cars except that after carving and sanding to finished shape, the inside of the body is hollowed out as necessary to fit over the chassis and motor unit. Gouge blades should be used in a modelling knife handle for hollowing out, removing only enough balsa as is necessary for clearance. This will leave the body as strong as possible for handling.

A method of attachment should be devised which holds the body securely in place, but also makes it possible to remove it again at any time for access to the motor or chassis unit for servicing. If possible, any attachment fittings required should be mounted on the body shell before it is finally sanded down and painted.

9 Scale Model Bridges

Bridge structures can readily be modelled in balsa strip and the resulting assembly can be surprisingly strong and rigid. Scale bridges built in balsa are quite strong enough to carry a model railway track and rolling stock, or form interesting scale models for making as display pieces. Construction is considerably simplified because of the ease with which balsa strip can be cut to length, and jointed strongly with quick-drying balsa cement. Small section balsa strip is also flexible enough to bend to curved shapes without having to steam or wet the wood first, and can readily be held in place with pins until the cement joints in a complete framework have set.

The simplest types of bridges are those known as *truss* bridges, where rigidity is provided by a series of frames designed to resist bending and twisting, as well as to carry a load distributed along the length of the bridge. Two identical frames form the two sides of the bridge, with interconnecting members to give the bridge the required width. Truss bridges are further classified as either *through bridges* where the roadway is carried by the bottom of the side frames and enclosed by the side frames and top struts; or *deck bridges* where all the framework is on the underside of the roadway (figure 9.1).

Through bridges are the most common type, and usually the simplest to build for short spans as well as giving the greatest clearance under the bridge. On smaller bridges the top strutting

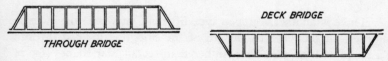

THROUGH BRIDGE

DECK BRIDGE

Figure 9.1

may be omitted. On larger bridges additional triangular braces may be added to the top struts to increase rigidity and resistance to twisting.

Deck bridges with multiple spans offer some savings for long bridges, with the individual spans supported on piers. They also, of course, give an uninterrupted view from the roadway, although this is usually of secondary importance only.

The secret of the strength and rigidity of a truss bridge lies in the design of the frames. Normally the length of the bridge is divided into an equal number of panels or bays, with uprights defining each bay. Simple rectangular frames like this are not rigid, and so additional bracing is added to make each bay stiff and resistant to deformation.

The two main types of braced frames used on full size bridges are the Pratt truss (figure 9.2) and the K-truss, (shown in

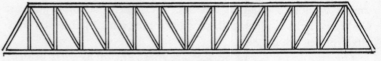

PRATT TRUSS

Figure 9.2

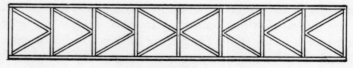

K-TRUSS

Figure 9.3

figure 9.3). In the Pratt truss a single diagonal bracing piece is used to stiffen each bay. In the K-truss, two bracing members are used in each bay, producing in effect a series of letter K's. Note how in both cases the pattern reverses at the centre of the bridge.

There is another common type of truss, known as the Warren girder. In this case the length of the bridge is divided up into a series of triangular bays, rather than rectangular shapes (figure 9.4). This may be rigid enough on its own. If not, additional

WARREN GIRDER

Figure 9.4

vertical struts are added in each bay. Then the resulting appearance is similar to that of the Pratt truss except that the diagonal braces run up and down, zig-zag fashion, along the length of the bridge instead of all being inclined in the same direction over each half span.

Model bridge construction

The side frames should be built first, assembled directly over a full size drawing. This drawing can be covered with waxed paper or rubbed over with the end of a candle, to prevent the frames sticking to the paper. Both frames should be built together, one on top of the other, to ensure that they are identical.

The plan must be laid on a flat working surface, such as a drawing board or a piece of flat wood soft enough to push pins into (hardboard or ply is no good). Failing anything else suitable, a piece of rigid corrugated card will do as a building board, provided it can be held down flat and true. The longer top and bottom members should be pinned down first in pairs (figure 9.5). If the balsa strip section used is smaller than 1/8" square, then pins

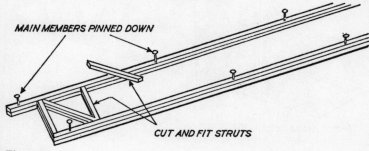

MAIN MEMBERS PINNED DOWN

CUT AND FIT STRUTS

Figure 9.5

should be placed on each side of the strips to hold them in place. Larger strip sections can be pinned right through without fear of splitting.

The individual upright members are then cut in pairs and cemented in place, working along the whole length of the bridge until two frames have been completed. Care should be taken to trim the edges of the balsa strip neatly so that each upright is a good fit, but not so tight a fit that the long members are pushed out of place. Double-cementing is recommended to give the strongest joints.

Frames should be left for an hour or more to set properly before the pins are removed and the frames lifted from the plan. The two frames will be stuck together and must be separated by running a thin knife blade, or razor blade, very carefully between them, working from one end to the other along each of the main members.

Joining the two frames is quite straightforward. The roadway can be cut from sheet balsa, pinned down over a flat surface. Each side frame is then cemented to the edges of the roadway and held in place with pins. A set square is then offered up to check that each frame is upright (figure 9.6). The top pieces can then be cut to length and cemented in place. All crosspieces will be the same length, so to ensure accuracy they should *all* be cut first

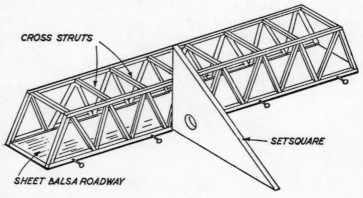

Figure 9.6

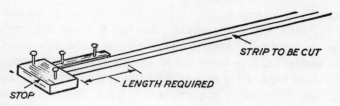

Figure 9.7

using one master piece as a pattern (see figure 9.7). If necessary these cross pieces can be held in place with pins until the cement has set, using the set square again to check that the assembly is square. Additional strutting should not be added until the main cross pieces have set in position.

Note that the same method of construction applies both to through bridges and deck bridges. In the latter case the bridge is merely assembled upside down.

Making scale bridges

You are not likely to find plans of actual bridges, so you will have to work from sketches or other illustrations found in books or magazines. From these it is a fairly simple matter to work out suitable proportions for height compared with length, and the spacing of the bays. You should also be able to identify what type of truss construction is being used.

Of course not all bridges will be of truss type. Some are rather more complicated, especially suspension bridges where the main framework is arched and the roadway is literally hung on cables. This will first need the construction of rigid towers from balsa sheet or sheet and strip, between which the main framework of strip can be fitted. The sheet balsa roadway can then be fitted, unsupported, and finally the cables (which in this case would be represented by thread of suitable thickness and colour).

Choosing a suitable scale can be quite difficult. Most of the better known bridges, and thus the most attractive subjects for modelling, are of considerable length. Selecting a scale to reduce the model length to a suitable size may mean that even the smallest balsa strip section readily available (1/16" square) is far too thick and out of scale. Also this is about the smallest balsa section strong enough to handle easily without breaking.

If smaller sections are required, these will have to be stripped from sheet balsa. 1/32 inch is the smallest sheet thickness available, and from this it is possible to cut any strip section from 1/32" square to wider sections with the same thickness. 1/32" square is about the smallest balsa section which can be handled properly anyway, so there is no point in planning to use even smaller sections. Thus the scale of the bridge should be selected accordingly, bearing in mind that on a fairly long model bridge the sections used can be quite a bit oversize in relation to true scale but still look right on the model.

The most satisfactory method of cutting strip from sheet is to use a tool known as a *balsa stripper*. This is really an adjustable guide for a modelling knife which can be run along the edge of the sheet to cut a strip equal in width to the setting of the guide (figure 9.8). It is also quite easy to make a balsa stripper from scrap wood and a razor blade, as shown in the second diagram. Use of a stripper ensures a continuous, even width cut from end to end of the sheet. It is virtually impossible to achieve anything like the same accuracy using a metal rule or straight-edge as a guide for the modelling knife.

Other types of bridges

Many types of bridges are built of brick or stone or reinforced concrete. In this case the whole of the structure can readily be duplicated in sheet balsa, suitably supported with strip framework on the inside, or at corners, as necessary, leaving the outside smooth and plain. This can be further decorated as necessary with more pieces of balsa sheet or strip, cemented in place, to produce a realistic replica of the full size subject.

In the case of stone or brick bridges, the outside surfaces of the balsa model can then be covered with brick or stone building paper, to the same scale. Alternatively, if suitable building papers are not available, suitable lines can be scored into the surface of

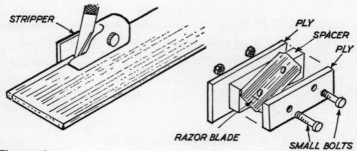

Figure 9.8

the balsa representing the positions of the original building blocks and the whole then painted in brick or stone colour. Emulsion paints are best for this for they will not roughen the grain of the balsa, also they will dry 'flat' without any gloss. Concrete bridges are even simpler to finish, for these can be painted over with a thin plaster of Paris mixture which will give a concrete texture to the whole when set (figure 9.9). Any

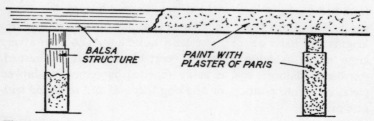

Figure 9.9

irregularities or lumps in the painted-on plaster coat can be flattened down by sanding with garnet paper.

Some scale model bridge subjects may demand more elaborate treatment. The bridge may again be built up from balsa sheet providing the overall shape and form required. The original stonework construction could then be represented with an overlay of pieces of thin balsa sheet, cut to suitable size and glued in place (figure 9.10). If the model can be laid on its side, these pieces can be prepainted and stuck down with PVA glue. Any surplus

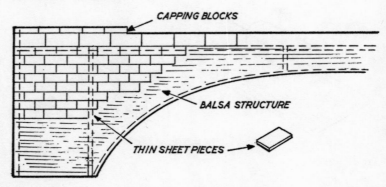

Figure 9.10

glue can then be wiped off without leaving smears on the surface.

Many other possible scale subjects for modelling use structures similar to bridges – a model of the Eiffel tower, for example. This could be constructed wholly of strip sections built up bit by bit – quite a task, but a challenge to any scale model enthusiast! Apart from being easy to use, balsa has two other advantages for elaborate models of this type. The total cost of materials required (strip lengths and balsa cement) is usually quite low. Also even a very large model is quite light and portable when it is finished. Accidental damage, too, is easily repaired by cementing broken pieces back into position, or breaking them off and replacing with new pieces.

10   Scale Model Buildings

Balsa is more suitable for the construction of model buildings than traditional materials, such as card. It is more rigid, can be cut to build up box shapes which can be cemented together without creasing and bending (which is necessary with card) and is altogether easier to work with.

All buildings, in fact, can be considered as built-up 'box' shapes – some simple boxes with four plain sides (walls) and a roof, others which can be broken down into a series of two or more box shapes joined together. And a box is a very easy subject to construct from sheet balsa.

The scale used should be chosen with care. Buildings are surprisingly large, especially when considered as a suitable match for a collection of other scale models. An ordinary house to 1/72nd scale, for example, will be about 5 inches long and 4 inches tall. And when it comes to lineside buildings to match model railways, a true scale size for stations, sheds, etc., is likely to be far too large to accommodate on an indoor layout. That is why model railway stations are usually drastically shortened, compared with full size, and platforms reduced in width, although they may be kept more or less true to scale in height (a reduction in height helps offset the lack of length and width). To fit in with other scale models as accessories, therefore, the proportions of model buildings often have to be adjusted from true scale dimensions. Model buildings made as separate scale subjects should be kept true to scale. Some examples of semi-scale buildings constructed in balsa are shown in figure 10.1. These are designed as accessories for model railway layouts, or scale model aircraft collections, and are extracted from the *Solarbo Book of Balsa Models*.

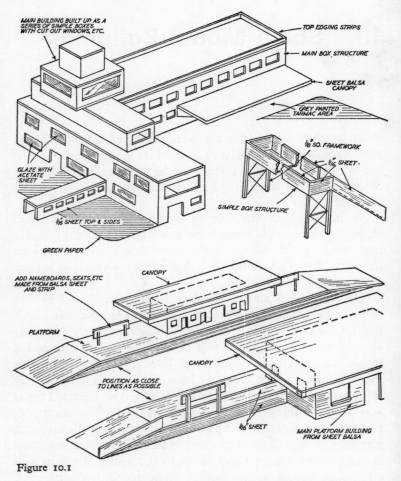

Figure 10.1

Basic model house construction is shown in figure 10.2. Sides and ends are cut out to shape from sheet balsa, with windows and door openings also cut out. 1/16 inch balsa sheet should be used for models up to about 1/96th scale. This is a minimum thickness for suitable strength and will also give a realistic scale thickness to walls at window cut outs. For 1/72nd scale walls should be cut from 3/32 inch thick sheet, and proportionately

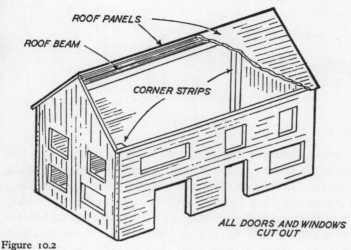

ROOF PANELS

ROOF BEAM

CORNER STRIPS

ALL DOORS AND WINDOWS
CUT OUT

Figure 10.2

thicker sheet again for larger scales, mainly to produce a strong
enough 'box'.

Inside corner joints for the sheet box should be reinforced
with pieces of balsa strip, cemented in place as shown. A further
piece of strip can be cemented between the two ends at the apex,
to act as a support for the roof pieces on models to 1/96th scale
or larger. This is not necessary on smaller scale models. The roof
pitch or slope angle is seldom exactly 45 degrees, usually less,
so the roof strip will have to be trimmed down to match the true
pitch angle before the roof pieces can be fitted. These again are
cut from balsa sheet, slightly oversize to overlap the sides and
ends. The top edges of the roof pieces also need chamfering or
angling off to fit together neatly.

Once the basic house 'box' has been completed it should be
covered with brick paper, or other appropriate building paper, to
the correct scale. Windows are cut out through the paper after
it is in position, allowing for an overlap which can be taken
through the cut-out, as shown in figure 10.3. This will hide
the cut edge of the balsa neatly and realistically. Alternatively, of
course, a model building can be finished in emulsion paint to

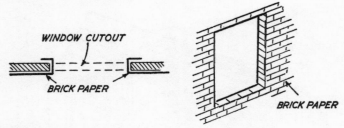

Figure 10.3

represent a distemper or colour wash finish or painted with thin plaster of Paris mixture to represent a rougher rendered surface, or concrete. No rubbing down after painting should be necessary.

Windows can then be completed by 'glazing' on the inside, followed by framing. For glazing, a piece of clear acetate sheet is cut to a suitable size to stick in place on the inside as shown in figure 10.4. Window frames are then carefully cut to fit. Here

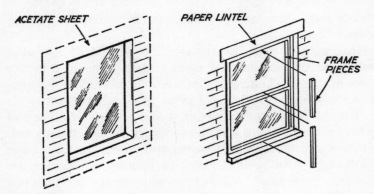

Figure 10.4

it is best to use a harder wood than balsa e.g., matchsticks, stripped down to a suitable section. Having cut them to size, the frames should then be painted and left to dry before finally gluing in place, using PVA adhesive or a water soluble gum. Any surplus glue can be removed with the tip of a damp paintbrush. The frame pieces are best held with tweezers for fixing them in the proper position.

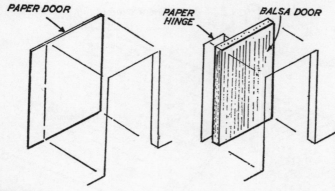

Figure 10.5

Doors can be of balsa sheet, or card. A card door is easy to hinge because a flap can be left for gluing the door in place on the inside and also to act as the hinge (figure 10.5). A balsa door can be hinged with a strip of paper. The advantage of a balsa door is that it can be a tight fit to wedge itself in place when pulled shut. A hinged card door will seldom shut properly. Whatever type of door is used it should be painted before finally fitting in place. In the case of a balsa door, a simple solution is to cover the front of the door with prepainted paper.

Other exterior detail can now be added to the model as required – e.g., see figure 10.6. Balsa sheet can be used extensively for building up porches, making chimney stacks, and so on. Guttering can be shaped by rubbing a narrow strip of stiff paper over a piece of wire to form it into a hollow shape. Brackets to carry the guttering should then be made from thin fuse wire, first secured to the underside of the edge of the roof with balsa cement and the guttering length then laid in place. Guttering can then be lightly gummed to the brackets. No attempt should be made to glue it directly to the edge of the roof as this will only pull it out of shape when the glue contracts on drying. Downpipes are best bent from aluminium or similar soft wire. They can be cemented in place at two or three suitable points along their length.

Full size house plans are readily available, showing all the

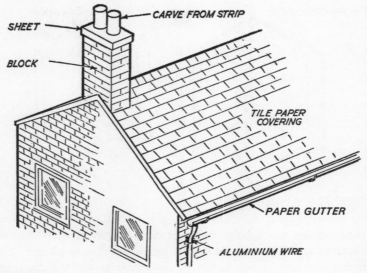

Figure 10.6

details necessary to reproduce a really fine scale model of almost any size. Your own house is a good guide as to the likely size of parts such as window frames, standard door sizes, and so on. What really makes a scale model house look right is having everything to scale. Real window frames, for example, are not 5 inches square, which is the size they would be if you used 1/16″ square strip on a 1/72nd scale model.

Other buildings can be tackled in the same way as model houses, thinking of them as basic 'boxes' with other shapes added on. Realism depends on three things:

1 Getting the shapes and proportions right, which really means working from a suitable scale drawing.
2 Incorporating a suitable amount of detail to the correct scale.
3 Getting a realistic finish on the model, with all the balsa hidden behind building papers or a suitable paint finish.

Good workmanship is also important. Bad joints or poorly finished balsa edges will show up through building paper coverings or paint. Any such defects should be made good before the paper or paint finish is applied. The same applies to all true scale model building. The job should never be hurried, and enough time, care and patience should be spent on it to make each part as perfect as possible – even the parts which do not necessarily show on the finished job.

The final appearance of a scale model building can also often be improved by 'ageing'. This means toning down the 'brand new' colouring of brickwork walls and tiled roofs, etc. Unfortunately this is not something that every modeller can do successfully, as a certain inherent artistic ability is essential.

Ageing effects are most readily produced by painting over the surface with a weak wash of a dull colour, or sometimes a very dilute stain. Water colour washes are probably best, for they can be removed with a damp sponge if the effect produced is not right. However, adhesion may be far from perfect, giving a blotchy appearance. There are really no hard and fast rules which can be followed. It is largely a matter of experimenting with different types of washes – preferably on scrap materials first – to find out what will best produce the effect required. Study actual buildings to see the natural discolorations and colour changes which do occur with age.

Table 6: Scale Brick Sizes

scale	brick size (inches)	suitable strip size for cutting bricks
$\frac{1}{8}$th	$1 \times \frac{1}{2}$	$\frac{1}{2} \times \frac{1}{4}$
$\frac{1}{12}$th	$\frac{3}{4} \times \frac{3}{8}$	$\frac{3}{8} \times \frac{3}{16}$
$\frac{1}{16}$th	$\frac{1}{2} \times \frac{1}{4}$	$\frac{1}{4} \times \frac{1}{8}$
$\frac{1}{29}$th	$\frac{3}{8} \times \frac{3}{16}$	$\frac{3}{16} \times \frac{3}{32}$
$\frac{1}{32}$nd	$\frac{1}{4} \times \frac{1}{8}$	$\frac{1}{8} \times \frac{1}{16}$
$\frac{1}{27}$th	$\frac{1}{8} \times \frac{1}{16}$	$\frac{1}{16} \times \frac{1}{32}$*

*stripped from $\frac{1}{32}$" sheet

11   Built-Up Models

The built-up model is the most advanced type of scale model construction. It is mainly used for flying scale aircraft, although a similar technique may also be applied to model boat hull construction. The basic aim with built-up construction is to duplicate as far as possible the 'skeleton' or framework of the full-size aircraft, the presence of which will still show to some extent on the completed model, adding to realism.

The advantages in this respect are limited to fabric-covered aircraft where rib and stringer positions show up through the covering material (usually tissue in the case of the model). For true scale effect, true scale rib positions and numbers of ribs, and true scale stringer positions are duplicated on the framework. In this respect the model construction follows the design of the full size airframe. Other internal parts which do not show may be modified for convenience, however, such as the use of formers cut from sheet balsa, rather than built-up frames which would be used on the full size aircraft.

Another advantage of built-up construction is that it can be kept light, which improves the flying qualities of the model. Also there is a lot of satisfaction in building a model which is true to scale (or nearly so) in airframe detail as well as outline shape and overall appearance, particularly for individuals who enjoy model *building*. Many built-up models of flying scale aircraft, in fact, are kept as display models rather than flown, the risk of damaging possibly hundreds of hours of work in a flight accident being regarded as too high. This was particularly true in the days when all flying scale models were rubber-powered, and their stability marginal. Only high wing prototypes usually make good rubber-powered flying scale models. The same is largely true of engine-powered free flight models. Scale models designed to be flown control line, or with modern proportional radio control, however, are far less liable to be damaged, and these are now the two chief types of flying scale model aircraft built. Mostly these are quite large models – some very large indeed – and choice of prototype is wide open . . . high wing, mid wing, low wing, biplane . . . single and multi-engined. Scale perfection is carried through in some cases to complete scale airframes, cockpit interiors and so on, sometimes involving 500 to 1,000 hours being spent on the actual construction of the model which would be worthy of display in any exhibition.

Built-up construction for model boat hulls would normally only be chosen by a modeller who wants to make a planked boat hull in the traditional manner – either clinker or carvel construction. The advantage of using balsa for the planking is the ease with which individual planks can be trimmed to shape to fit properly. Balsa is specially applicable for planking smaller hulls, say up to about 24 inches long. For larger sizes a harder wood would normally be preferred for greater strength.

Built-up scale aircraft

The most complicated part of the airframe of a built-up flying scale model aeroplane is the fuselage. This is usually of rounded shape, with a number of thin sectioned longitudinal members or *stringers* running from end to end, supported on a basic framework, or formers.

Former construction is usually the simplest for this means that the former shapes can be taken directly as cross sections, spaced at suitable intervals along the fuselage length. If mounted in a suitable manner, say on a central member, a rounded fuselage shape can be completed by mounting stringers directly on to these formers (figure 11.1). These stringers can also follow changes of shape or section readily because they are of thin strip. At the same time the formers must be spaced fairly closely together to give the stringers sufficient rigidity. The resulting fuselage structure is thus very much more complicated than a simple square

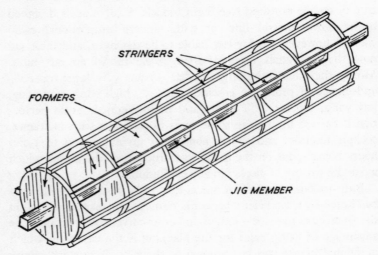

Figure 11.1

' box ' frame built from balsa strip, such as commonly employed for non-scale flying model aircraft. It is also heavier, but not necessarily so much heavier as to detract seriously from the flying performance of the model.

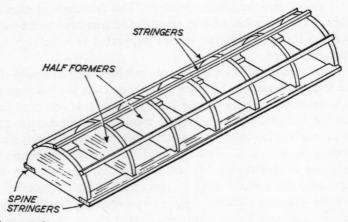

Figure 11.2

The weight is to some extent governed by the limiting material sizes which can be employed. 1/16 inch sheet is about the minimum thickness which can be employed for formers, and this will need increasing in the case of larger models. For the stringers 1/16" square is a minimum size. Again this may need increasing in the case of a larger model.

There is, therefore, a sort of ' optimum ' size where 1/16 inch thick formers and 1/16" square stringers provide the best combination of weight saving and necessary strength. This generally applies to models between about 24 and 36 inches wingspan. Any smaller model size is penalized by the question of added weight, since it must still use these minimum wood sizes. Larger models work out better since the wood sizes can be adjusted upwards as necessary for strength, without necessarily increasing the weight in similar proportion.

What this really means is that designing a scale model airframe for built-up construction is a skilled job, requiring plenty of experience to know what best to do. The most satisfactory way of tackling such a project is to build from a published plan of a proven design, or from a kit if available. This at least will avoid the possibility of making serious mistakes which could lead to structural weaknesses, or an overweight model which will never fly properly. An overweight model does not necessarily mean that it will be stronger. In fact, a flying scale model which is overweight is far more likely to suffer serious damage from a crash landing than a lighter one. It will not fly so well – and it will hit the ground that much harder!

The construction of flat frames, such as wings and tailplanes, presents no particular problems. These can be built flat over a full size framework, as with simple frames. The only difference is the additional number of parts to be fitted up and their closer spacing, calling for more precise workmanship.

Fuselage assembly can be simplified to some extent by splitting the formers into halves, normally vertically. A set of half formers can then be erected directly over a side view drawing and a half shell completed by adding the stringers (figure 11.2). Once this assembly has set it can be removed from the plan and the other set of half formers mounted on the other side, followed by the second set of stringers. The original half shell will be rigid enough to resist any distortion.

Half shell construction is usually more accurate than working with full formers assembled on a central member. In the latter case the stringers usually have to be fitted up in opposite pairs to prevent a warp developing. Also they are usually more difficult to align properly.

Half shell fuselage construction for flying scale model aircraft originated with a range of kits produced in the United States during the 1930s. At this period most full size aircraft were still of fabric covered construction, fully justifying this method of reproduction in miniature. This particular range of kits virtually established as standard for built-up construction for flying scale model aircraft of full size designs before the all-metal stressed skin era. Although the kits themselves are no longer in production, plans of all the original models have recently become available again, and have been added to and extended to cover new models. They are the ideal reference for anyone interested in flying scale models.*

Many aircraft fuselage shapes, of course, lend themselves to other forms of built-up construction on scale lines. Material sizes cannot be kept to scale – 1/16" square is a minimum size for balsa stringers, for example – but this does not generally matter. If the same form of construction can be employed the result will still appear realistic.

The following diagrams and notes can be studied as a guide to possible treatment of a particular prototype chosen. Scale frame and stringer positions should be adopted on fuselages, where these show on the finished model (e.g. in the case of a fabric covered fuselage). Similarly with fabric covered wings, where scale rib positioning should be adopted. Where the prototype has large sheeted areas (covered in ply or metal, for example), construction can often be simplified by the extensive use of sheet balsa.

*Cleveland Model and Supply Co, 10307E Detroit Avenue, Cleveland, Ohio, U.S.A.

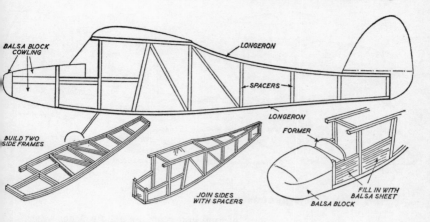

Box frame fuselage construction

Many full size aircraft have a 'box' section fuselage based on a built-up frame-work of longerons and spacers. This type of construction can readily be duplicated in balsa, using scale spacer positions, etc., if desired for complete authenticity – e.g. where framework would normally be expected to show up through 'fabric' covering.

Basis of such a construction is shown above. First two identical side frames are built, preferably one on top of the other, pinned down flat over a full size plan. These are separated and joined with spacers to complete the basic framework. Additional strutting, etc., can be added as necessary. Solid panels, such as provided by sheet metal or plywood covering on the full size prototype, can be duplicated by filling in between appropriate frame sections with sheet balsa. Alternatively a plywood covered fuselage could be duplicated by covering the framework with thin sheet balsa.

With built-up box frame construction, longerons and spacers in balsa are almost invariably square in section – 1/16" square for fuselage lengths up to about 12 inches; 3/32" or 1/8" square for fuselages up to 24–30 inches; and 3/16" or 1/4" square for larger fuselages. Additional strutting can be smaller sections to save weight. Tissue covering is suitable for all smaller models. Very large models are best covered in silk or nylon.

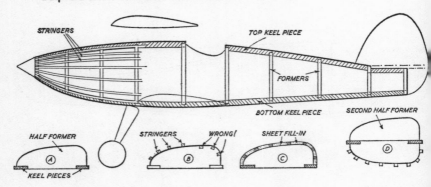

Half shell fuselage construction

This is the classic method of building scale model fuselages where the section is rounded or streamlined. Top and bottom pieces are cut from sheet balsa to conform to the profile shape of the fuselage. These are pinned down flat over a full size plan. Former shapes are carefully plotted and cut out in sheet balsa. Each former is then cut vertically into two half formers. One set of half formers is cemented in place to the keel pieces, after which stringers are added to complete a built-up 'half shell'. When set, this is removed and the other set of half formers cemented in position. The fuselage is then completed by adding the stringers on this side.

Detail A shows how the formers should be split so that the first set of half formers can be notched to fit over the keel pieces. Note from detail B that the stringers should be cemented on top of the half formers, not notched in flush (this will produce ridges in the fuselage covering). 'Solid' sections can be represented by filling in with pieces of soft sheet balsa between stringers (detail C).

Use 1/16 inch sheet for formers, except for larger models. Stringers should be 1/16" square for models up to 24 inches long; and 3/32" square for larger fuselages. Use closely spaced formers to prevent stringers 'sagging' when the fuselage is covered and doped.

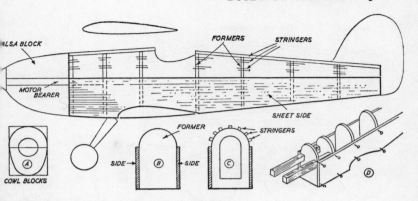

Sheet side and former construction

This is suitable where the fuselage is basically slabsided with a rounded top (or bottom). Sides are cut from sheet balsa, but only to the depth of the flat or 'slabsided' section. A complete set of full formers is then cut from sheet balsa and assembled between the sides (detail B). The fuselage shape is then completed by adding stringers around the protruding part(s) of the formers (detail C).

Note that where the front of the fuselage is rounded, this section can be tackled separately by carving from solid balsa blocks which are attached later to the main fuselage assembly.

It is usually possible with this type of construction to assemble the first three or four formers directly to the two sheet balsa sides, holding with pins until set (detail D). After checking that this assembly is 'square' the remaining formers can be added, and the two sides joined at the extreme rear. With some fuselage shapes it may be necessary to start by joining the two sides with the middle two or three formers and then work to each end in turn.

An alternative method of construction, which is lighter, is to make the 'slabsided' part of the fuselage in the form of a built-up box framework, adding formers to the top (and/or bottom), and then complete with stringers.

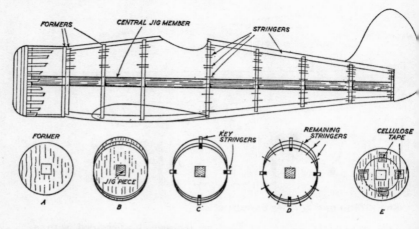

Jig type fuselage construction

This method uses full formers which are assembled on a central jigging rod, sufficiently rigid to resist bending. Stringers are then cemented in place to the formers, after which the jigging rod can be withdrawn. This type of construction relies very much on accurate plotting and cutting of the former shapes.

Formers should be cut for a tight fit in the jigging rod, which should be square or rectangular in section (detail A). All the formers are then assembled on the jig, in turn, and accurately positioned (detail B). Four (or more) key stringers should then be assembled, locating in notches in the formers (detail C). These key stringers must be of rectangular section (e.g. 1/8″ x 1/16″ where the rest of the stringers are 1/16″ square). After checking that the assembly is true, the remaining square section stringers are then cemented in position to the outside of the formers (detail D). To avoid any possibility of distorting the fuselage, assemble these stringers in opposite pairs.

Note that if the formers need to be cut out (e.g. to pass a rubber motor, or to save weight), the centre of each former should be cut out and then replaced and held with cellulose tape (detail E) before mounting on the jigging rod.

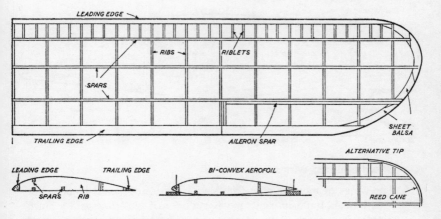

Built-up wing construction

For a fabric covered wing this should be based on scale rib and spar positions. The wing should be drawn out full size, in detail, and the framework assembled directly over the plan. Ribs and riblets should be cut from 1/32 inch balsa sheet for models up to about 24–30 inches span. For larger models 1/16 inch sheet will have to be used to eliminate buckling.

Leading and trailing edges should be preshaped before pinning down over the plan. Curved tip shapes can be cut from sheet balsa, split into several parts to avoid cross grain. Alternatively, tips can be bent from reed cane or thin bamboo sections.

One problem which may arise is that wings with a bi-convex aerofoil section cannot be pinned down flat over the building plan. In this case both the leading and trailing edge members must be blocked up clear of the plan to allow the ribs to be positioned properly.

Wings are generally best built as separate panels, subsequently joined together at the correct dihedral angle (with braces at the spar joints). A wing with no dihedral should be built flat as one continuous frame. Dihedralled wings can also be built in this way, notching the spars at the centre to form to dihedral after the complete structure has been built and has had time to set.

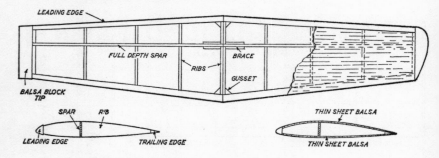

Sheet covered wings

The wings of most modern (full size) aircraft are metal skinned. For scale models, built-up construction can be used, this time with a much simpler framework. After joining at the correct dihedral the top and bottom of the wing is then covered with sheet balsa.

Short cut methods are often possible. For example, if the wing is flat bottomed in aerofoil section the wing plan shape can be cut from sheet balsa and the framework built directly on this. Finally the top sheet covering is added.

Sheet covered wings tend to be heavy, so use the slightest balsa sheet available for a flying model. This sheet is not suitable, except for very small models, as it will tend to sag between the ribs and spars. Use 1/16 inch sheet and sand down *before* cementing in place. This will both reduce its thickness slightly (saving weight) and minimize the amount of finish sanding necessary. Heaving sanding on sheet covering will tend to work right through the sheet at rib and spar positions.

Tailplanes, fins and rudders

These are nearly always best made as built-up frames, like wings. They can be tissue covered (to represent fabric covering), or covered with presanded 1/32 inch sheet balsa (to represent metal covering). On small models, or where weights is not important, 'metal covered' tail surfaces can be cut directly from sheet balsa, sanded down to section.

12 Miscellaneous Subjects

One of the more unusual applications of balsa is for figure modelling. The material is quite strong enough for carving figures up to about 12 inches high and offers the following specific advantages:

1 Ease of carving to shape.

2 The possibility of building up the basic figure from separate blocks. This not only simplifies the work involved, but enables basic proportions to be reproduced accurately.

It should be pointed out that figure modelling is an art rather than a modelling craft. In other words it needs a certain inherent ability on the part of the modeller to produce realistic scale figures as all the final shaping is freehand. Ordinary models are a different position. Anyone can learn to reproduce realistic and accurate scale models, merely by following mechanical techniques. Thus figure modelling is quite different from ordinary scale modelling. However skilled a modelling craftsman may be, it needs something extra in the way of artistic ability to produce good scale figures.

Starting point is to break the figure down into basic shapes. Figure 12.1 shows this applied to a human figure, each part derived as a straightforward geometric shape of correct proportions and with *natural pivot points*. The proportions shown are those of an average male figure with a height of 5 ft 10 in. It can be adapted to an average female figure, and to other heights.

In planning suitable proportions for different heights it should be remembered that differences in human figure heights are due mainly to differences in *leg* (and arm) length. The head and trunk proportions on a 5-foot adult may not be very different

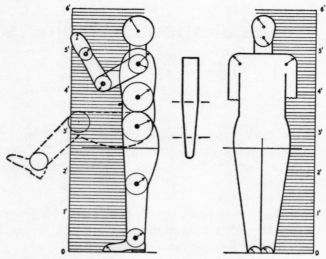

Figure 12.1

from those of a 6-foot adult.

Cutting out the basic shapes in thick card or thin sheet balsa, and joining at pivot points with paper fasteners, will produce a useful scale model template. This can be adjusted to a realistic attitude, as in figure 12.2, and will be an invaluable guide to assembling a basic figure from block.

The block shapes required follow the same breakdown as that of the template figure, namely:

        Head
        Neck (this is additional to the template parts)
        Upper trunk
        Abdomen
        Lower body
        Upper arm (two)
        Lower arm (two)
        Hand (two)
        Upper leg (two)
        Lower leg (two)
        Foot (two)

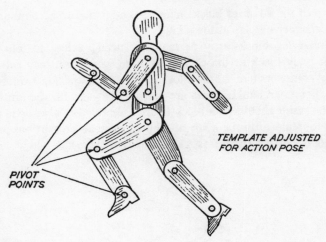

TEMPLATE ADJUSTED
FOR ACTION POSE

PIVOT
POINTS

Figure 12.2

All these parts have the same outline shapes as the figure template (figure 12.1), and thus the same positions for the pivot points. This time, however, they are cut as solid rather than flat pieces, with thicknesses derived to the same scale from the other drawing given in figure 12.1.

Having cut all these parts, the problem then is to assemble them to complete a basic block figure, using the template as a guide. This time the various parts cannot be pivoted together, but have to be suitably jointed.

Start with the body first. For a fully upright figure the three blocks are simply cut with square ends and cemented together. For any other attitude it will be necessary to trim the ends of the body blocks to give the required 'displacement' about the appropriate pivot point(s). Similarly, the required attitude of the head is given by trimming the neck block.

The upper arm blocks are usually no problem since these can be cemented directly to the body at the shoulders. The lower arms will have to be half-jointed, however, to give the required bend at the elbow. Similarly, the hand will have to be half-jointed to the lower arm at the wrist. Note that in this case the length of the adjacent blocks may need adjusting to accommodate a satisfactory overlap at the joint.

Upper leg blocks may or may not need angling to join the lower body block at the correct attitude, and again may call for some adjustment of initial block length to allow for trimming. Knee joints and ankle joints are half-jointed, as with the arms.

The result should be a block figure assembled in a realistic and true to scale attitude, with all the individual proportions substantially correct (figure 12.3). Up to this stage the whole cons-

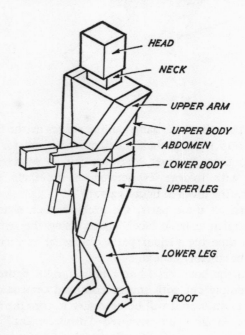

HEAD

NECK

UPPER ARM

UPPER BODY

ABDOMEN

LOWER BODY

UPPER LEG

LOWER LEG

FOOT

Figure 12.3

truction has been mechanical scale modelling. No artistic ability is involved. The final work, however, demands a flair for sculpture – reducing the figure by carving to a realistic human shape. The block figure is essentially a *blank*, rendered in the simplest possible form for final shaping by carving.

A similar technique can be extended to the carving of animal figures, although balsa is less suitable as a working material here where slender components may be involved, e.g., thin legs. The resulting proportions can be too fragile for handling, or even carving properly. Animal subjects, in fact, are usually best treated in 'solid' attitudes, such as lying down, where legs are not separate carvings. The whole figure can then be carved, or literally sculpted, from a solid block of balsa. This then becomes a complete art form subject. The only real advantage offered by balsa for such work is that it is easy to carve. Also mistakes in carving can readily be rectified by cementing back a piece removed in error and proceeding in a matter of a few minutes as soon as the cement has set.

Balsa has also been used with considerable success for making models of insects and similar living subjects. In this case the scale chosen is normally larger than life, with 'mixed' construction for the final model. Thus only the more solid parts are carved from balsa. Legs are bent from wire, suitably covered and finished, wings from transparent sheet plastic, suitably veined and lined, and so on.

Where mixed construction is employed, additional materials should be chosen to be compatible with balsa cement for ease of assembly. Thus aluminium wire will 'take' balsa cement, iron wire less well. Cellulose acetate or cellulose nitrate (celluloid) is also readily stuck with balsa cement. Polystyrene is not stuck with balsa cement, and expanded polystyrene is attacked and dissolved by balsa cement. Paper and other woods are also suitable for jointing with balsa cement.

A further possibility with scientific or educational model construction is the making of skeletons. These can be life size, or to a larger or smaller scale, according to the subject chosen. A full size working drawing is first prepared, which is then studied to see whether individual bones are best cut from strip (straight bones with a minimum of shaping), or sheet (curved bones, such as ribs). Skulls can be carved directly from block, or again built up from sheet parts and finally carved to shape.

The scope here is quite considerable. For demonstration purposes the skeleton model can be diagrammatic, or to simplified scale, or fully detailed to scale. In the former case all the individual bones are included, but not shaped in detail, or even exactly correct in outline. With a fully detailed or true scale model, every individual bone is fully shaped to scale proportions before being assembled.

Figure 12.4 shows a much simplified skeleton model of a toad. Starting point is a base block, which can be balsa sheet,

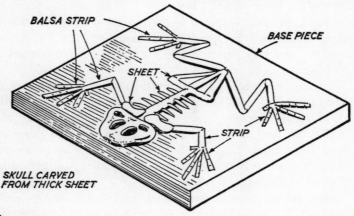

Figure 12.4

cut to a suitable size, smoothed and painted with sanding sealer and finally painted matt black. The skeleton is then built up bit by bit from sheet and strip parts, all to scale size and length, the degree of shaping used being a matter of personal preference. These parts are cemented down either to the base board, or to each other, as appropriate. No colouring is needed as the natural colour of balsa is sufficiently bone-like. This avoids the tricky operation of sanding and sealing small, fragile balsa parts. If colouring is thought desirable, however, this can be done with poster paints.

Relief maps

The construction of relief maps to a small scale is another subject for which balsa is well suited. Starting with a base panel of hardboard or ply, individual contour patterns are cut from sheet balsa and cemented in place. The thickness of the balsa sheet used is decided by the scale of the map – see Table 7 page 118.

The complete 'stepped' assembly should then be left for at least 12 hours for the cement to dry thoroughly (figure 12.5) It

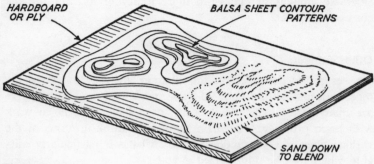

HARDBOARD OR PLY

BALSA SHEET CONTOUR PATTERNS

SAND DOWN TO BLEND

Figure 12.5

can then be sanded down to blend the contour layers into each other, making sure that all joint lines are smoothed right off. The glasspaper can be wrapped around small curved blocks of balsa, or even a finger, to work in natural curves. The whole surface can then be treated with sanding sealer and further rubbed down as necessary.

A balsa relief map produced in this way readily lends itself to adding further detail. Where appropriate, this can be scored into the surface. The whole can then be finished in a suitable ground colour or colours. Texture can also be added to the surface if desired. For example, areas can be painted with gum and sprinkled with sand or balsa dust and the surplus blown off when dry. Water can be represented by pieces of perspex sheet cut to shape and inset in the balsa.

If necessary, further detail can be added to the model after painting. Blocks of buildings can be represented by pieces of balsa strip, suitably shaped and painted before being glued down in place. PVA adhesive is better than balsa cement for this job since it will not smear and any surplus glue can be removed with the tip of a dampened paint brush before it has set.

The advantage offered by using balsa for scale model relief maps is that a high degree of accuracy can be achieved. Contours can be accurately duplicated, both in shape and height. The alternative method of building up a relief map in plaster or some similar modelling medium over a base normally involves a considerable amount of 'guesstimation' in trying to duplicate the correct contours.

Other subjects

The examples described in this chapter are only a few of the more unusual applications of scale modelling in balsa. There are many others which will occur, once having learnt to work with balsa properly. The main thing is to think in terms of the various types of construction for which balsa is particularly suitable, which may be summarized as under:

1 Solid scale modelling, where the basis is first to produce a suitable *blank* from solid block, or basic assemblies of blocks or block and sheet balsa. This is then carved and finished down to the actual solid shape required.

2 Box-type assemblies constructed from balsa sheet. This is particularly adaptable to the construction of scale model buildings, etc. Boxes do not have to be rectangular in shape. They can be built up in sections as necessary, to arrive at virtually any shape.

3 Framework assemblies, where the full size object to be modelled itself consists of various frames. These may be open frames, as in bridges, or covered frames, e.g., as in the case of built-up scale model aircraft. Built-up construction is adaptable to the widest variety of shapes, using sheet balsa parts as formers, and strip sections for building up the shape around the formers.

4 Sheet construction, where smooth surface subjects can be duplicated from sheet panels, suitably joined together and reinforced with internal frames or braces, as necessary. This is really a variation on box-type construction.

5 Authentic construction, where balsa is used to duplicate a specific construction in miniature, taking advantage of the ease

with which even intricate assemblies can be completed in balsa using quick-drying cement. Examples include the use of balsa strips for planking a model boat hull in the same manner as full size construction; or the use of scale size bricks cut from strip balsa for true-to-scale brickwork assemblies.

6 Time-saving, where balsa can be used to produce a mock-up or *blank* from a simple construction of sheet, strip and block, which can be finished off in various ways to complete the final scale shape required. This can represent a considerable saving in time over built-up construction where it is the finished result which is important rather than the detail construction.

7 Simplifying techniques. The use of balsa, which can be worked satisfactorily with no other tools than a sharp modelling knife or razor blade and a small fine-tooth saw, means that you can work on balsa modelling practically anywhere. Also assemblies can be completed quickly, using quick-drying cement, and holding joints in place until set only needs the use of pins.

8 Ready availability. Balsa is a material which is readily available, not at all expensive, and is normally stocked by all model shops in a wide range of sizes. Non-standard strip sizes can easily be cut from sheet, using a balsa stripper, and large section balsa block is very easy to saw down to smaller block sizes.

Remember also, that although balsa is not as strong as other woods it is very strong for its weight. Practically all the balsa sold through model shops is kiln dried, which means that it is fully seasoned and durable. It is the most versatile of all modelling materials.

Table 7: Contour Thicknesses

Scale		100 feet	200 feet	500 feet	1000 feet	
$\frac{1}{3000000}$					.003	
$\frac{1}{2000000}$					.006	
$\frac{1}{1000000}$					.012	$(\frac{1}{64})$
$\frac{1}{500000}$				$\frac{1}{64}$	.024	$(\frac{1}{32})$
$\frac{1}{250000}$	(A)		$\frac{1}{64}$	$\frac{1}{32}$	.05	$\frac{3}{64}$
$\frac{1}{125000}$	(B)	$\frac{1}{64}$	$\frac{1}{32}$	$\frac{3}{64}$	.095	$(\frac{3}{32})$
$\frac{1}{63000}$	(C)	$\frac{1}{64}$	$\frac{1}{32}$	$\frac{3}{32}$	.19	$(\frac{3}{16})$
$\frac{1}{32000}$	(D)	$\frac{1}{32}$	$\frac{1}{16}$	$\frac{3}{16}$	.375	$(\frac{3}{8})$
$\frac{1}{16000}$	(E)	$\frac{1}{16}$	$\frac{5}{32}$	$\frac{3}{8}$	.75	$(\frac{3}{4})$
$\frac{1}{8000}$	(F)	$\frac{5}{32}$	$\frac{5}{16}$	$\frac{3}{4}$	1.5	$(1\frac{1}{2})$

(A) Approximately $\frac{1}{4}''$ to mile
(B)   ,, $\frac{1}{2}''$,,   ,,
(C)   ,, $1''$,,   ,,
(D)   ,, $2''$,,   ,,
(E)   ,, $3''$,,   ,,
(F)   ,, $4''$,,   ,,

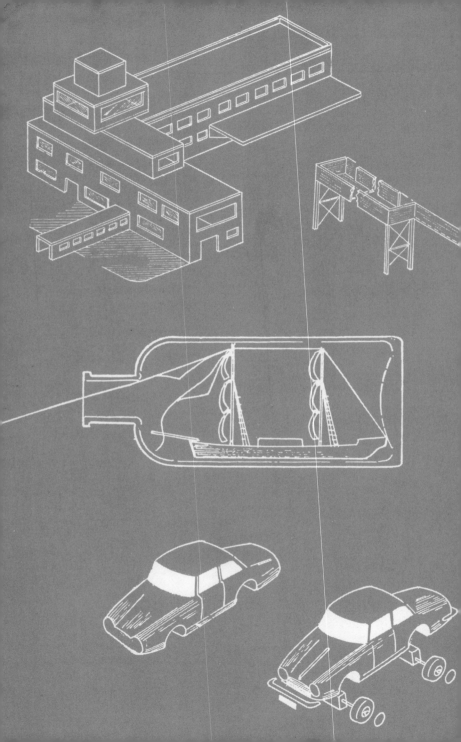

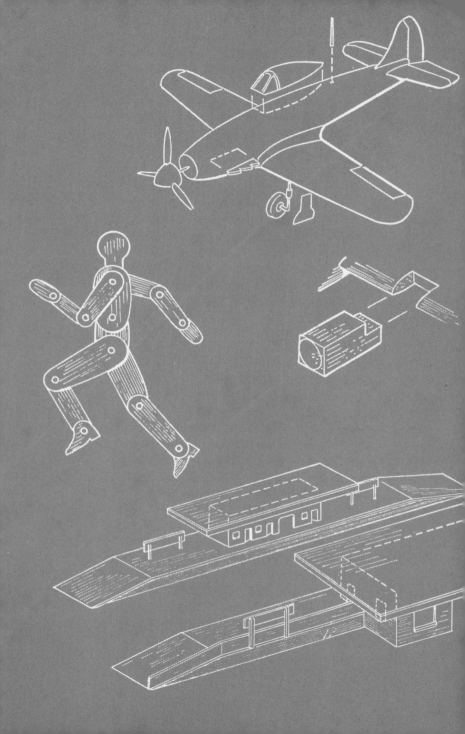